space
planning

space planning

Designing the Office Environment

LILA SHOSHKES

ARCHITECTURAL RECORD BOOKS
New York

The editors for this book were Martin Filler and
Patricia Mintz.
The designer was Elaine Golt Gongora
The production supervisor was Susanne LanFranchi.
It was set in Avant Garde Book by Design Type, Inc.
The printer was the Halliday Lithograph Corporation.
The binder was the Book Press.

Library of Congress Cataloging in Publication Data

Shoshkes, Lila, 1926 -
    Space planning.

    Bibliography: p.
    Includes index.
    1. Office layout.   I. Title.
HF5547.S525   658.2'3   76-41305
ISBN 0-07-057060-4

Published by Architectural Record,
A McGraw-Hill Publication,
1221 Avenue of the Americas,
New York, New York 10020

"The reality of a building consists not in the walls and the roof, but in the space within."
Lao-Tse

To Carol, Ellen, Ann and Deena,
for a life beyond planning.

contents

In the past, books about the planning and design of offices generally fell into two categories. One described the practical problems of "how to." The second presented office design in beautiful photographs of handsome installations. Up until now, there has been very little discussion of the critical issues that underlie planning and design decisions. Such a lack of self-examination may be attributed to the rapid growth of the field.

Recently, designers and management have begun to examine the elements that comprise the work environment. What is emerging is a new and unique realization — that the space planner, whether architect or interior designer, is part of a management consulting team.

Interest in the critical issues that have been the concern of the space planner has been shown in a number of ways. There have been several seminars and courses given at universities such as Harvard and the University of Wisconsin for design professionals. Numerous seminars organized by management magazines have attracted large audiences of management representatives. This reflects the needs of this special group for more information. Magazines that designers read have addressed themselves with increasing frequency to specialized topics of space planning.

This book is concerned with examining the basic problems of design and planning with regard to the growing body of knowledge of how people work and the changing technologies of the office. It is an expanding subject with contributions from a host of consultants in the social sciences, hardware, acoustics, computers, lighting, paper flow, and audiovisual fields. The aesthetic, functional, and psychological aspects of the office have become very specialized subjects in a relatively short period of time. Because it is a serious subject for examination and study, the office offers a creative challenge to designers and architects.

The problem of putting people and furniture in space does not exist in a vacuum. Pragmatically, the furniture and space in our buildings are not ideal. Buildings constructed for tenants may work well for small firms such as lawyers and insurance companies, but may be unsuited for large users of space who might be a single tenant of a floor or more. The architect cannot be a hero to both kinds of users. If management decides to build its own facility, can designers suggest the ideal space for that purpose? Designers are still learning about space. They are learning about how large and unlimited a space can be before we feel it is too large. We still cannot say what the most comfortable and efficient size of space would be to work in, 8,000, 20,000, or 40,000 square feet.

Implementing ideas with furniture that is available has led to frustrations. The furniture systems that have been developed are less than ideal. Some lead to arrangements that are in direct opposition to the nature of open office planning. The furniture often dominates the space, creating honeycombs, roomettes, or mazes, cutting of contact and communication.

This book owes its origin to a suggestion by a colleague who is actively engaged in space planning. He wanted and needed to know more about what he was actively doing. If this book bears only a limited resemblance to what we originally discussed, I can only cite my own shortcomings. I must express my indebtedness to Saul Anton for opening this area of inquiry.

I have learned from the experience of others who shared their knowledge with me in frank and open discussions. Partly because some discussions were off the record and partly because I prefer to write on my own authority, the book represents the distillation of many experiences, presented with a minimum of attribution to individuals. I have also searched the libraries of the American Management Association and Avery Library at Columbia University, and I am grateful for the background they provided me. Plans and details of individual offices have, for the most part, been excluded. I did this because I felt that "one should hear the song before one reads the score", as Lionel Brett, a writer on architectural subjects has said.

I want to express my thanks to all those people who helped with this assemblage of information. I am particularly indebted to them for their cooperation, experience, and for the photographs that illuminate my poor prose. I only regret that I had to limit myself to the few design firms represented here. I wish that I could have included the work of many others whose excellent design work deserves recognition.

This book could never have been written without the tremendous encouragement and unfailing support of my husband, Milton.

CHANGING TIMES

Design, the expression of our material culture, is a product of our collective identity. The image it reflects can be regarded as a historical fact and as a hard won solution to our problems. Our solutions accumulate and problems alter but we can look back and see our development through design.

The development of space planning came as a response to the problems of corporate growth. This growth gave impetus to an already existing field. As planning needs expanded, new specialists and specialties developed.

Between 1950 and 1960 the expansion of business created an office building boom throughout the world. As businesses proliferated, large corporations found themselves with their management scattered in many locations. Towards the end of the fifties this management dispersal resulted in a new phenomena — the development of corporate headquarters.

Corporate headquarters brought together large numbers of people into one space. Before this, typical tenants in an office building occupied at the most, several floors in that building. Now an entire office building was being used to house just one company. This made it possible for the company to control its construction to suit the company's needs. They began to be concerned and aware of the office as a work environment.

There were other changes in the architecture of office buildings at this time, as well. After World War II ended and materials became available, the development of year-round air conditioning and uniform lighting became possible. We were able to end dependence on natural light and ventilation. Office buildings of the twenties and thirties were tall, shallow structures, designed to give maximum exposure to exterior windows. Now the inner areas of buildings became usable for work areas. Office buildings with large unbroken floor spaces became practical. Zoning changes allowed speculative builders to get maximum rents from expensive urban properties.

Corporations brought large numbers of employees to work in these monolithic spaces. This meant a radical change in how this space was used. The new buildings and new user demands required new solutions for the problems of people working in these spaces.

PIONEERS

In the Thirties, a few architects, industrial designers, and display designers had been aware of how poorly businesses were utilizing office space. In the Forties and Fifties they were joined by creative people from other disciplines. Given the opportunity to design a working environment to fit the needs of companies, a few architects and designers began to examine the basic questions of how people work and how the office can be designed to meet their needs. These few people, pioneers in interior design, responded to the needs of the time. They were the catalysts and conduits of a whole complex of ideas associated with modern architecture, modern management, and modern design. Architects, interior designers, graphic artists, display and industrial designers, and a few manufacturers of contemporary furniture were stimulated by the great need for their contribution at this seminal time.

In the forties there were only two manufacturers of contemporary furniture — the Herman Miller Company and Knoll Associates. They both realized that they would have to show people how to use their furniture. Their showrooms became very influential in educating architects, designers, and their clients.

Jack Dunbar, now an Associate Partner in Interior Design at Skidmore, Owings and Merrill (S.O.M.), designed all of Herman Miller's showrooms during the mid fifties. Before that, he had had a variety of experiences searching for what was right for him. After a couple of months at the Frank Lloyd Wright Fellowship and a semester at the Chicago Institute of Design, he came to New York and worked as a photographer's assistant and in graphic design. For three years he was the art director at Harpers Bazaar, before he started to design showrooms. When he joined S.O.M. in the late fifties, it was at a very exciting time. There was a sense of optimism. There was change in the atmosphere at the start of something that did not yet exist — dealing with clients who were open to new ideas.

Florence Schust Knoll, studied at Cranbrook and the Architectural Association of London. She completed her architecture degree with Mies van der Rohe at the Illinois Institute of Technology. After meeting Hans Knoll and joining his staff, she started the Knoll Planning Unit in 1944 to handle its interior design operations. During the fifties and sixties the Knoll Planning Unit became very influential in corporate design work. Many people now at the heads of their own firms, such as Louis Beal of ISD in New York, can trace their beginnings back to the early days at Knoll.

The history of space planning should mention the contribution of others, such as J. Gordon Carr, Sidney Rodgers, George Nelson, Donald Desky, and Michael Saphier. Only a full scale history of the period would do justice to the others who contributed.

Among the first design firms to specialize in the working environment was Designs For Business, Inc., started by Maurice Mogulescu. He had come to New York to study law but found himself interested in display construction for the New York World's Fair of 1939. Display work developed into designing showrooms. After the war ended the new design firm, Designs For Business, Inc., took shape and began to grow.

Gerald Luss, now a partner in Luss, Kaplan and Associates, Limited, joined Designs For Business in 1948. He had studied architecture. "We were given design problems, but we were designing shells. If ever we were concerned with interiors, it was always an afterthought." Frustrated with his architecture education, Luss went to Pratt Institute. A course in interior design was being offered for the first time by Konrad Wittman, former state architect of Austria, who had fled just as Hitler came to power. Wittman believed that the interior governed the shape of the eventual architecture.

Wittman and other teachers who had fled from Europe were an important influence for many young students then. Several people from the Bauhaus left Germany and were teaching at Brooklyn College, under the chairmanship of Serge Chermayeff. Lawrence Lerner found himself studying pure Bauhaus design philosophy at the end of the war. In 1948 he joined Michael Saphier Associates as a designer. The company name changed in 1962 to Saphier, Lerner and Schindler Environetics, now known as SLS Environetics.

The introduction of Bauhaus ideas affected art and architecture education. It caused a turning away from the traditional beaux arts approach. Such a design education was available at universities where the intellectual climate stimulated and changed the emphasis to one of investigation and problem solving. This caused a shift from the classic tradition of studio art training, which had emphasized the art of the past.

BEGINNINGS

The contribution of this stimulating and varied group of young people to the problems of designing office spaces in the Fifties helped to crystallize interior design. Space planning became a dynamic process that was not taught in any school. It developed as a response to the needs of the time.

The unique approach of space planning — that of a dynamic problem-solving process used for the office environment — can be seen, for example, in S.O.M.'s seminal Union Carbide headquarters of 1959 and Designs For Business's design for Time Incorporated. The concepts of total flexibility, interchangeable modular parts, and systems thinking has remained basically unchanged.

The Union Carbide headquarters provided the opportunity to develop partition systems (Fig. 1), a furniture system that permitted desks to have interchangeable pedestals (Fig. 2), and an integrated filing and storage system (Fig. 3). It marked the first use of clustered work stations with low dividers (Fig. 4). Lighting, air conditioning, and the partition system are integrated with a 5-foot grid, keyed into the ceiling runners. The runners support the ceiling, lock in the partitions, and act as continuous strip diffusers. There was no need for fire stops or sound baffles since the space above the plastic ceiling was divided into modular cells, each enclosing a light fixture.

The problem-solving approach used for Time, Incorporated developed the idea of systems thinking. The Time offices gave Designs For Business the opportunity to design a totally flexible modular interior system that integrated ceilings, lighting, air conditioning, and an easily demountable wall partition.

These installations provided an opportunity to design literally everything that went into these buildings and shaped the building to meet the client's needs. The revolutionary nature of the offices described here can be appreciated when seen in rela-

Fig. 1. **The detailing of office spaces in the Union Carbide headquarters, reflected the systems thinking of the ceiling and partition systems. It was the first time carpeting was used continuously throughout an office building.**
Courtesy Skidmore, Owings and Merrill)

Fig. 2. **The desks at Union Carbide were designed by Skidmore, Owings and Merrill to reflect the structural system that was being used in the building. It marked the first use of this desk design that was to be copied all over the world. The pedestals had interchangeable modular components.**
(Courtesy Skidmore, Owings and Merrill)

5

Fig. 3. **A standardized storage system was developed and used throughout Union Carbide. It was the first time banks of five-drawer high files were used and coordinated with cabinets.**
(Courtesy Skidmore, Owings and Merrill)

Fig. 4. **The use of clustered work stations with low partitions was developed first at Union Carbide as an innovative solution to planning pool areas also using banks of five-drawer-high files for dividers.**
(Courtesy Skidmore, Owings and Merrill)

tion to what was then considered the most impeccable office building yet designed — the Seagram's Building of 1958. Its curtain wall construction rigidly imposed a 20-foot band of luminous ceiling around the perimeter that fixed the size of all offices on the window walls. The Seagram's Building imposed these restrictions on its users, just like the other office buildings that were being constructed at that time. However, in the Time Inc. and Union Carbide headquarters, the users were able to satisfy their needs for flexibility for the first time and the use of space reflected the way people worked.

The concept of flexibility evolved as designers were called back by clients to cope with expansion problems and changes in operations. This concept was based not on the assumption that changes would occur but on the certainty that every department would be affected.

When Time Inc. selected Designs For Business to design their facility, they were faced with the certainty of change. There were the constant expansion, contraction, and changes in organization and operations of their various magazines. Time Inc. was remodeling its layouts so often that the average life of a partition was 1.4 years. This was at a tremendous cost in labor efficiency due to disruption as well as the cost of the partition. Designs For Business estimated the initial cost of the partition at about $15 a lineal foot, for a gypsum-block partition. Add to that $5 to $6 for demolition at that time, and the removal of rubbish, and add another $15 to erect a new partition. That amounted to $36 a lineal foot for a partition that was moved every 1.4 years.

Designs For Business tried to produce maximum flexibility by reducing the number of elements that had to be moved when changes occurred. They evolved a total system based on a single module on which the building was finally built. Each module contained its own air conditioning, lighting, acoustic environment, electrical and telephone facilities. None of these elements had to be moved or changed, except to replace a burned-out light bulb. The facilities were always there and always available. It utilized a modular partition that could have a desk top hung from it, as well as cabinets, shelves, and task lighting. In short it had everything that was needed for a person to sit down and perform his or her function.

THE QUICKBORNER TEAM

The demands for change that gave rise to the pioneer installations at Union Carbide and Time Inc. in New York City were also being felt in Europe. In post-war Hamburg, two brothers who had fled from East Germany found the bombed-out city busy rebuilding. A tremendous demand for office furniture existed. They were the sons of a man who had a factory that manufactured office equipment before they had fled from the Russians. With his sons' help, the father started anew in Hamburg. They quickly found that management did not know what its needs were and needed advice before they could order furniture. They established a consulting service, called the Quickborner Team. They severed their connections with the sale of equipment to avoid a conflict of interest, and concentrated on the study of office systems. (It is interesting to note that Knoll also had a planning unit. Because of similar problems of a conflict of interest, Knoll terminated their planning unit in 1970.)

The Quickborner Team also stressed the need to facilitate communications and paper flow, ideas they felt could best be expressed in an open office layout. They reviewed the equipment that went into the office and decided that smaller, lighter desks and open basket files would improve the paper flow since paper would not be stored at a work station. It provided an easy way, they felt, to supervise work flow.

Their first big project was for the largest publishing firm in Germany. They had an innovative approach that employed experts from many fields who worked out a methodology that was completely unique at the time. They brought together acousticians, physicists, psychologists, and systems people. Out of it came the concept of office landscaping that was to have such a far-reaching effect.

"It was a blessing and a curse," said Dr. R. E. Planas, the president of the American office of the Quickborner Team. "The blessing was that the term and the whole thing made us famous. The drawback is now we are labeled as office landscaping artists, so that people feel they cannot involve us in any other way."

THE IMPACT OF OFFICE LANDSCAPING

Office landscaping, as a concept of planning, had an international ripple effect even where no examples of its application existed. In 1962, magazine articles began appearing describing the very rigid dicta that were then held. Office landscaping was surrounded by clouds of mystery and obscurity, complicated by the idea that it must be accepted as a totality or that it wouldn't "work."

The kernel of truth in the system, was profound enough to have world-wide impact: Office layouts should not be bound by fixed walls but should reflect the fact that small working units of people interact all the time with many other units. To facilitate such interaction and to speed communications, people should have unimpeded proximity to each other. In order to delineate areas or provide some open screening, plants were used in profusion, hence the term "landscaping."

At first, the layouts showed scattered, nongeometric patterns based on acoustic theories and with some idea of avoiding eye contact among employees to control possible distraction. The scattered pattern seemed to be the most unsettling and irritating aspect to many people who voiced objections. People used to private offices and geometric layouts found it chaotic visually. Generally, the use of random layout has faded but the memory lingers on.

Open planning, the term most generally used, had a strong impact in America where it caught on more readily than in Europe. The open office concept has not been as accepted in France as it has in England and in the areas where the German language facilitated the introduction of the Quickborner Team's ideas. Except for drafting rooms, Europeans, with a few exceptions, have not had large offices up to this time. America had the tradition of using the bull pen layout and a greater openness in communications, compared to Europe where the executives and managers traditionally sit in closed door offices, accessible through a corridor from their closed door secretaries.

Woodie Holstein of the Port Authority of New York and New Jersey recalled his first exposure to the Quickborner Team. "I went to a meeting at the General Electric offices in New York.

A corporate official of General Electric was hosting a meeting of people from large organizations in the metropolitan New York area to introduce new and radical ideas about interior office design. People from Chase Manhattan, IBM, and half a dozen others were there to hear the Quickborner Team's ideas. They opened our eyes to the open office idea."

Clearly, open planning was an idea whose time had come. It strongly influenced furniture manufacturers, who responded with a great variety of furniture. The dynamism of the industry's involvement was greater than in Europe. At first the emphasis was on the Quickborner Team's concept of lightness, openness, and small scale. Herman Miller became convinced it was the way to go and began adapting their furniture to respond to what they felt to be a tremendous interest in this country. They started their planning unit, the Design Resource Service.

What the Quickborner Team has done has been to introduce to the design profession and the users the theory that there are more barriers built up and more isolation in partitions than is necessary. More and more firms have come to realize that in the open office they are able to satisfy their need for more flexibility, and that flexibility is probably the single most important factor in building and planning today. Both the German management consultants and the American designers were working towards the same conceptual breakthrough. They had the same goal — to let the space reflect the way people need to work.

chapter two
designing
for
people

A MAZE OF THEORIES

Does design affect the people working in offices? Management is interested in how productivity may be affected, while psychologists are interested in the effects on individual and group behavior. Still others are interested in quantifying and understanding the experience that is created or influenced by our designs.

How people work has traditionally been the concern of management. The factors that influence people in the organization have been studied and measured. For the designer, it is a more recent concern. This chapter will put the findings of management, behavioral scientists, and social psychologists into a framework to help guide designers through the maze of theories.

Designers looking for facts and theories that can be directly applied to their work will find the material elusive. User research has failed to meet the real needs of designers. It has neglected the fact that people are adaptive and not passive recipients in the environment. The perspective that this study gives is that the findings of theorists have little impact on space planning and design. There are no clear-cut conclusions that can be useful in developing a design theory. However, provocative and important ideas about our environment have come from research being done by the National Aeronautics and Space Administration (NASA). They have posed some very basic, disturbing questions that will be discussed at the end of this chapter.

The effects of the environment on pepole are being discussed and studied from many points of view. It was the concern of the International Design Conference in Aspen which had as its theme "Dimensions of Experience." Writers in design and architecture magazines have been dazzling their less knowledgeable readers with words like "ergonomics," "proxemics," and "ekistics." These are the catch words of theories about human behavior being applied to the study of the office environment. They represent the relationship between individual and individual, individual and space, and individual and object. Other writers are concerned with advocacy planning and transactional analysis, human factors engineering, and the social aspects of the office. They describe how people come together to interact and share experiences — the "social waterhole." Work output is thought by these writers to be a product of social activity.

While there are very few guidelines for design and planning, the developing body of knowledge about work, working, and the worker has created many useful tools of research. Designers are using these tools to understand management and to gather information for planning. The results of that research has added to our knowledge of ourselves but has yielded little concrete information to aid in developing a design theory.

UNSCRAMBLING MANAGEMENT THEORY

Behavioral scientists, using involved language, have constructed complex theories explaining the nature of management. Many of their theories have a common theme. A very simplified list of these common themes about human resource management would include these points:

1. An optimistic view of employees assumes a belief in each individual's desire for self actualization.

2. The talents of most people are wasted by the way we structure and manage our organizations.

3. The failure to utilize talents and skills makes work an unsatisfying experience, and we suffer psychological damage to our sense of well-being.

4. This failure makes the organization less effective than it could be in utilizing human talent for the greatest economic effectiveness.

5. Management needs to restructure the work experience to meet the needs of the employees and increase the organization's economic effectiveness.

These assumptions are drawn from the theories of analysts of management philosophy, like Peter Drucker, Frederick Herzberg, Rensis Likert, Abraham Maslow, and Douglas McGregor. These theorists have developed technics that they feel contribute to solving the problem of poor integration of the needs of the individual and the organization. Some of these technics are familiar to designers. In space planning, designers use some of them as a way of understanding the organization and as methods of gathering information. The technics fall into two broad categories.

1. Diagnosing problems by information gathering — using surveys and interview studies, training needs analysis, human resource accounting, job/work flow analysis.

2. Diagnosing problems in the way people interact — using job enrichment, job enlargement, matrix organizations and semi-autonomous work groups, participative decision making, transactional analysis, team building, management by objectives.

STUDIES OF WORK AND WORKING

The study of the individual and work began at the end of the 19th Century with Frederick Taylor. He laid the foundation of systematic observation and study. An early example of the search for meaningful design criteria in the qualification of behavior was the experiments of Elton Mayo and his associates called the Hawthorne Studies. These experiments measured the impact of changes in the light levels on the performance of workers assembling and testing telephone equipment. The conclusions, called the Hawthorne Effect, state that any change in the environment will produce a temporary increase in productivity.

All the studies of work and working are based on measuring human performance and attitudes. The quantification of human behavior in work situations starts with the physiological aspects of workers and their environments, such as lighting and vision fatigue studies, tool design, temperature conditions in the environment, and individual aptitudes. It is sometimes referred to as anthropometry or Human Factors Engineering. This area of study represents a vast amount of research.

An excellent bibliography of much of this source material was compiled by Walter Kleeman, Jr., an Associate Professor of Interior Design at Western Kentucky University, for the Council of Planning Librarians, entitled "Interior Ergonomics — Significant Dimensions in Interior Design and Planning. He gives the definition of Ergonomics from the Ergonomic Research Society of England. It is the study of the relationship between a person and his or her occupation, equipment, and environment. It is concerned with the application of anatomical, physiological, and psychological knowledge to the problems arising from this relationship. The title suggests that there are significant dimensions in interior design. A careful reading of his introductory essay and the material listed shows that the "significant dimensions" refers to the dimensions of the problem not of the solution.

Ergonomics is part of the social, biological, and behavioral study of Industrial Psychology and Human Relations and is concerned with individuals and groups at work. Peter Drucker, the respected authority on management analysis, in reviewing the results of these studies, has concluded that the totality of work, worker and working, task and job, perception and personality, work community rewards, and power relations may be far too complex to be truly understood.

STUDIES OF PERSONAL SPACE

The studies about the environment and human behavior that deal with conversation, crowding, territoriality, seating arrangements, and cultural messages about space can be loosely grouped under the heading of **personal space**. There have been many studies about seating arrangements in relation to stimulating conversation, affecting leadership recognition, affecting isolation and alienation, and/or encouraging interaction.

These studies of personal space give the designer many interesting isolated observations. For example, the behavioral scientist E. T. Hall has investigated personal and transactional space and has stated that for an Arabian the normal distance for conversation is where one can smell the breath of another person; for an American, this would be much too close for conversation. How people position themselves and maintain distances between themselves and others has been referred to by Hall as their "proxemic relationship."

Another interesting study on personal space involves the effects of crowding. Jonathan L. Freedman, professor of psychology at Columbia University, says that crowding intensifies people's normal reactions to a situation. If they ordinarily respond positively, they will be more positive under crowded situations that increase excitement, stimulation, and friendliness. If people are negative, they will have more fear and antagonism.

Some discussions about personal space deal with the idea of territoriality. It has been observed by psychologist Robert Sommer that people create barriers to define territory. They use their posture or location to convey this idea in a "silent language." It borrows from the biologists' notion of animal territoriality based on mating, feeding, and nesting and applies the term to a noninstinctual pattern.

Design can give clues for behavior by sending culturally understood messages about expected responses. We all know how we are expected to act in a church, library, ball park, or bus station. Psychologists recognized that seatless toilets, security hardware, and other aspects of institutional life conveyed to patients how the hospital personnel think they will behave and the patients oblige by regression and loss of control. In other reports, dramatic changes were noted when carpet is installed in place of tile. Patients become less irritable, employees modulate their voices, and there is a decrease in vandalism.

THE PROBLEM OF MEANINGFUL DATA

Kleeman, in his bibliography, lists several articles published by the Aerospace Medical Research Laboratories, reflecting their concern about designing for people in space. They were trying to develop meaningful design criteria from these studies to apply to the Space Program. The Aerospace Medical Research Laboratory studies showed that some basic data could not be developed into design criteria. For example, K. H. Eberhard-Kroemer reviewed European literature for them on the ergonomics of office furniture and healthy sitting postures. The body postures of sedentary workers has always been a concern of orthopedists and physiologists. He found that although medically and anthropometrically oriented researchers can point out main principles, their recommendations do not concur and are not sufficient for either a definition of "healthy" or "good" sitting postures; or for establishing design standards for chairs.

One reason it is difficult to get meaningful data is that people are complex and adaptive, making ongoing adjustments in their reactions to the environment. This was emphasized by Dr. Jon Rogers, Dean of Humanities and Behavioral Sciences at the University of Alabama, in a thoughtful research paper for the National Aeronautics and Space Administration (NASA), "Environmental Needs of Individuals and Groups." He concludes that people adapt to their environment rather than creating an environment to suit their desires.

The different stresses of psychological, physiological, social, and economic conditions push and pull. The different elements can be isolated, measured, and analyzed, but as Mr. Eberhard-Kroemer says, researchers cannot even agree on what is healthy or good for a relatively easily isolated and measurable component.

As people's needs are met, they change in the act of being satisfied. Designers handling so many variables are faced with having to emphasize some needs and not others. They hope continually to find a key factor. Every survey or study reported raises the designer's hopes that at last he or she will have the data to find out what to do.

RESPONDING TO THE ENVIRONMENT

We have not yet been able to answer the serious question we brought up at the beginning of this chapter. The question of how design affects the individual working in the office may very well be the wrong question. By asking that, we are looking for a simple connection between environmental features and the responses of a person in that environment.

Constance Perrin, in her very stimulating book, "With Man in Mind," points out that people working in a space develop adaptive behaviors that cannot be expressed as a theory about the space. The quality of human interactions and interpersonal relationships is a function of non-spatial and non-physical variables. She feels what is missing is a theory of human nature that is unique to environmental design. This must include the strivings of people for equilibrium in their personal and social needs and for that which maintains and extends their sense of confidence and self-interest.

In addressing this problem, Dr. David Nowlis has contributed a most meaningful analysis. Dr. Nowlis has raised serious questions that have troubled all designers. In his research for NASA he questioned the underlying notion that "good habitability response came from good setting design." He had reservations because of some obvious exceptions. First, why is it that some seemingly poor environments, such as run-down communities, may have many vigorous well-disposed residents who preferred that community to other seemingly well designed, efficient, and more supportive communities? Second, he wondered why highly successful business people who worked and lived in plush surroundings were happiest when vacationing in crude cabins in the woods with no design quality at all. Third, he wondered why poor housing was correlated with high crime rates and a high incidence of mental and physical illness in some cities and countries and not in others.

These exceptions provided Dr. Nowlis with the single most important direction research has taken in uncovering an outstanding psychological factor in the process of human response to the environment. Dr. Nowlis feels the impact of sensed freedom and dignity in the environment, room for individuality, a sense of value and purpose, and a sensed freedom of choice dramatically effect how a person deals with the external environment, no matter how beautiful or crude it is in design.

Three components of this factor are: individuality, a sense of purpose, and a sense of choice. They overlap as people interact with their environment. We can all contribute examples from our own experiences to illustrate this insight.

For designers the lessons are clear, and clearly this is the direction that planning has been taking recently. The needs of individuals, the designer's concern for their requirements, and the involvement of them in the design process all work to reinforce the sense of purpose and the sense of choice that go to make the design a success and the environment supportive. It is an ongoing involvement, starting with the planning process. There are valuable tools to help the continuing dialogue, such as information programs, the use of mock-ups, newsletters, and introductory seminars. Whatever a designer can do to involve the people in the evolution of the new space adds to the value of the space. Without this attention one can count on the instant self-destruction of a beautiful design, like a Tinguely sculpture.

chapter three
management
and the
space planner

THE SELECTION OF A CONSULTANT

Before the period of expansion of the fifties, the problem of adapting to new space or expanding an existing space might be in the hands of office managers who ordered furniture and rented space with some occasional help from a craftsman and builder. They would tell them what they thought they needed and they would move people and furniture into the rooms available. Faced with the open spaces available in office buildings newly built since the fifties, this simple solution could no longer be used. Both the nature of business and the housing of it had changed.

Buildings are now designed with huge amounts of interior space. The office manager was no longer able to cope with the complexities. The landlord required that the person laying out the space submit a set of plans to be included in the lease. This involved the integration and organization of the layout with the lighting design, air conditioning, underfloor ducts, telephone and intercom distribution systems, and ceiling systems. All these factors and more were beyond what the office manager could be expected to deal with. As a result management has become increasingly aware of the value of space planning and more knowledgeable about working with planners and the design community. Space planners were able to provide management with a major tool — the collaboration necessary to adapt the organization to the new working conditions.

The General Services Administration (GSA) has started a design improvement program. The GSA's Public Building Service (PBS) is the agency that designs and constructs Federal building. The PBS is responsible for finding the land, hiring the professional to design and build it, the contract documents, the award and supervision of the contract up to and now including interior design and space planning. It was a major step for the GSA and the PBS to incorporate interior design and space planning as a discipline into their total design concept for new major renovations or lease construction. One of the first projects to benefit from this program is the Interstate Commerce Commission for 300,000 square feet of space planning.

The way a large organization seeks a space planning consultant has become very sophisticated and knowledgeable. It reflects the systematic decision-making approach that they use in other management operations. For example, when, in 1964, the Port Authority of New York and New Jersey anticipated moving its administrative offices into about 500,000 square feet of space in their World Trade Center, they used a carefully planned approach for the selection of a consultant. They were looking for planners who could demonstrate their ability for space planning of this magnitude. To accomplish that, they established a set of performance standards that they expected their consultants to meet or exceed. They invited consultants to submit proposals based on six planning concepts that the Port Authority developed. These were: review of the master plan, establishment of long-range space requirements, evaluation of spacial studies, development of block layouts, and lastly, design of detailed layouts. These were all developed with the Port Authority staff.

The Port Authority then rated the proposals (Table 1), and the past performance of the consultant as provided by their references (Table III). Each item had been given a numerical value by the Port Authority's Organization and Procedures Committee (Table II). Decision was made by a thorough analysis of the consultants' abilities, their proposals, their references, and planning costs. They awarded the contract to Ford and Earl Associates of Warren, Michigan.

The selection process is not foolproof. Collaborations do not always work out as anticipated. This example is cited to show how management can use its tools for decision making.

While the selection process does not always guarantee a successful collaboration, collaboration, to be a success, must depend on close client contact. Close contact with a client is critical and vital to the whole design process. The dialogue between the planner and the people in the organization is the only way of gaining vital information. The knowledge of how a particular organization works is essential, and the planner must make his or her own observations. "There is no substitute," said Jack Dunbar of S.O.M., "but to move in and observe, down to the last paper cup. Then you have a feel for it as a human being. The client and the dialogue are crucial for the job."

Table 1. **RATINGS OF PROPOSALS**

To assist the Port Authority in selecting a design consultant, the Authority developed this form to analyze rate proposals.

(Courtesy The Port Authority of New York and New Jersey)

ITEM	DESCRIPTION	AVAILABLE POINTS	AWARDED POINTS	REMARKS
1.	Completed One Major Job (300M - 10 fls)			
2.	Major Jobs Completed Since 1960 (5 pts. ea.)	150		
	Personnel Assigned With Necessary Skills And Sound Experience (Maximum of Project Leader, 2 Principals, 1 Senior)	150		
	Quality of Work Shown By Attachments (Request Samples If Not With Proposal)	50		
3.	Performance	(550)	- - -	Check max. of 4 clients
	Met Deadlines	50		
	Followed Proposal	-		
	Assigned Indicated Staff	20		
	Followed Plan That Had Been Outlined	30		
	Final Cost Approach Estimate	50		
	Job Is Of High Quality	100		
	Long Range Projections Appear Accurate	50		
	Worked Well With and *For* Client's Staff	50		
	Did Consultant Voluntarily Follow Up On Project to Assure Satisfactory Perform.	100		
	What Are Consultant's Strong & Weak Pts.	20		
	Any Problems With Consultant - What	20		
	Would You Re-Hire For Similar Job?	50		
	Did Client Have Experience With Personnel To Be Assigned (Check Against Item 2)	-0-	- - -	
	How Consultant Work With Client Archt.	10		
4.	Understands Our Problems (Does Not Repeat)	50		
	Details A Realistic Approach	200		
	Proposes Realistic Time Schedule	50		
	Proposes A Realistic Manning Table With Own and PA Staff	150		
	Evidences Creativity and Flexibility	50		
	Proposed Quality Studies Not Included In Master Plan	100		
	TOTAL	1,500		

Table 2. **REFERENCE EVALUATION**

The Port Authority developed this form to evaluate the references of design consultants. It supplements the information given in Table I to aid in management decision making.

(Courtesy The Port Authority of New York and New Jersey)

REFERENCE CHECK

CONSULTANT _____   TOTAL SCORE _____

FIRM: _____   CONTACT _____

I. **Size of Job:** (minimum of 5 floors, 100,000 sq. ft.)
       _____ floors   _____ sq. ft.

II. **Method of Selection**   (5)
   (5)   _____   1. competitive bidding via submittal of written proposals
   (1)   _____   2. competitive bidding via oral proposal
   (0)   _____   3. selective invitation

III. **Type of Job** (Must include Building Profile)   (10)
   (10)   _____   1. developed building profile, including block space allocation considering environmental, organizational and operational problems.
   (5)   _____   2. developed building profile including block space allocation only
   (0)   _____   3. layout work only

IV. **Personnel Projections**   (10)
   (6)   _____   1. developed or reviewed long-range (5 yr.) personnel projections
   (4)   _____   2. developed or reviewed space standards
   (4)   _____   3. had to accept client's projections (but questioned and/or tested validity)
   (2)   _____   4. had to accept client's standards (but questioned and/or tested validity)
   (0)   _____   5. chose to accept projections
   (0)   _____   6. chose to accept standards

V. **Space Allocations**   (30)
   (10)   _____   1. developed personnel space requirements from projections and standards
   (5)   _____   2. allowed for expansion personnel space
        _____   3. specialized areas   (10)
          (3)   _____   a. eating facility
          (1)   _____   b. lounge area
          (3)   _____   c. storage areas
          (2)   _____   d. executive area
          (1)   _____   e. parking area
   (5)   _____   4. allowed for expansion for specialized areas

VI. **Special Requirements**   (20)
   A. Materials handling   (13)
     (10)   _____   1. developed or reviewed client's materials handling system
     (3)   _____   2. recommended innovations
     (5)   _____   3. forced to accept client's specifications (but recommended changes)
     (0)   _____   4. chose to accept conventional building system

   B. Communications System   (7)
     (5)   _____   1. developed or reviewed clients communications system
     (3)   _____   2. forced to accept clients' specifications (but recommended changes)
     (2)   _____   3. recommended innovations
     (0)   _____   4. chose to accept conventional system

VII. **Layout Work**   (10)
   (5)   _____   1. service was provided
   (5)   _____   2. service was of high quality
   (3)   _____   3. service was of average quality
   (0)   _____   4. service was inferior

RATING OF PROPOSAL FROM _____

ITEM	DESCRIPTION	AVAILABLE POINTS	AWARDED POINTS	REMARKS
1.	Completed One Major Job (300 - 10 floors)			
2.	Major Jobs Successfully Completed Since 1960 (5 points each)	150		
3.	Understands Our Problem (Does Not Repeat)	50		
	Details A Realistic Approach	200		
	Proposes Realistic Time Schedule	50		
	Proposes A Realistic Manning Table With Own and PA Staff	150		
	Evidence Creativity and Flexibility	50		
	Proposed Quality Studies Not Included In Master Plan	100		
	TOTAL			

Table 3. **NUMERICAL EVALUATION**

The Port Authority was searching for a design consultant who had demonstrated ability in space planning large facilities. By giving numerical values to information gathered in other forms, various consultants could be compared.
(Courtesy The Port Authority of New York and New Jersey)

THE DYNAMICS OF CHANGE

Whether by careful planning or by intuitive decision, when management decides to make a change and expand their facility, it usually comes at a time when confidence is strong. The decision helps direct the company to define realistic goals. The company's objectives are clarified and the need for change is carefully examined. This self-examination adds strength to management as it becomes critically aware of the best way to serve various competing interests within the company.

The first step is for management to evaluate carefully whether expansion is really necessary before large sums are allocated to detail planning and construction. The company gathers and analyzes the information it knows about itself and tries to develop a long-range plan. Frequently, management consultants and other specialists are called in to contribute outside opinions before a firm decision is made.

While striving to establish realistic goals the company is, at the same time, indulging in daydreams and fantasies. The company collectively has a dream of the ideal — a wonderful ordering of people, money, and space. In this Utopia everyone will have an Eames chair, a parking space, and the trains will always run on time. These fantasy wishes create an unrealistic handicap even before a planner starts. The dynamics of change lies in the reconciling of the ideal and the real.

Ultimately the responsibility for long-range planning rests with the chief executive officer. He or she and the principle policy makers make the plan work.

THE RESISTANCE TO CHANGE

There is resistance implied in planning. There is resistance to new ideas generally. Richard Bauer, at AT&T, described one aspect of it very well. "Our people are busy with their very specialized responsibilities. We get our people from operating companies for two or three years, very high-level staff people who make major management decisions. They do not understand our job and they don't have time to think about it. If you start changing things, say if you are going into a space where there are no windows or you are going to be in an open office, if you are going to be in an open landscape, this requires them to take time from what they are paid to do, their job, and it's troublesome."

The deep-rooted need for the private office in executive territory is a hard won symbol that can be very threatening to have removed. When AT&T was planning to move its new facilities to Basking Ridge, New Jersey, open planning was considered for executives in the early stages of the design. When the people who were actually going to use these spaces realized what was planned for them, they refused to be deprived of their walls. They came from companies where many of them had been supervising five hundred to seven hundred people with a nice private office. When a man has worked fifteen to twenty years of his life for a company, he doesn't want to give up any of the prestige items. AT&T values its executives and their needs and the plan was changed to suit them.

People resist change and resist being changed by planners. Change involves the unknown and the unknowable, and it is accepted with great reservation. Change can be seen as a threat. Not only is there resistance to new ideas, such as at AT&T, there is resistance to change.

Planned changes alter a company. Some people in the company may see it as changing the stability of team relations in departmental politics. It can bring feelings of tension, suspicion, stress, and resistance.

Change can also generate an informal group feeling. Such a group may react in a conservative fashion to resist the planner. This group feeling is reinforced by the feelings of the individual members who are reluctant to change. Members of this group relate to each other because of these shared feelings about the "outsider" or the threat of change.

In some instances designers have experienced a process in which the implementers subvert the intention of the originally approved presentation. It might not be a resistance to change but rather a bureaucratic "interpretation" of method that can produce difficulties. In Jack Dunbar's words, "Bureaucracy sometimes takes over and changes are made without referring back to the approving boards or committees. In such instances the design or scheme is slowly eroded through the change of shape, form or color. It's a most frustrating experience when it happens, because one leaves the project feeling that the service isn't proper in view of the fact that the presented scheme has been lost."

Constraints that develop because of internal politics or unconscious reaction can limit open communication. Power and political situations may cause managers to ignore and distort information to accomplish their own goals which are to move ahead in the organization or build their own empire. In addition, they are in a position to distort the flow of information upward or downward, often only reporting information that will protect them. As one designer explained it, "There are frustrating situations where we are prevented from doing a proper analysis by getting the data needed. That seems to go together with the kind of organization where you make your proposal, that theoretically everyone agreed with, but is subverted."

Every plan, well drawn or not, creates resistance. Planning creates anti-planning. This basic human phenomena crops up in man-made delays, vague manifestations of discontent, or lapses in administration. All of which are symptoms of a death wish applied to organization life.

COMMUNICATION AND INVOLVEMENT

Another constraint to planning that can be a serious consideration is the interpersonal relationship between the planner and the client. Most people deny that a constraint exists, but there is no intimate relationship without some unexpected strain. The existence of emotions is not recognized in the official world of design. The design and architecture magazines give the impression that we live in a beautifully planned, beautifully resolved environment, unclouded with any mention of emotional involvement. In contrast, management has recognized and given an important place to the role of emotions in communications between people.

The interpersonal relationship between the planner and the client places them each in a dependent position. They depend on each other for information and they must receive assistance from each other to perform. Being dependent can raise unconscious emotional reactions, unexplained by real circumstances, mixed with feelings of anxiety. The vulnerability, anxiety, and discomfort people feel is often hidden. What they express is a feeling of defensiveness and anger. More barriers are created to hide this emotionally difficult situation from themselves and others. Defensiveness can hinder the dialogue and collaboration.

Space planners faced with the problems of coping with these constraints, objections, and unconscious resistances have learned that recognition of the problem is important. Simple methods can be used to mitigate the forces of opposition directed at the space planner. By using communication and involvement, the planner and management must attempt to keep an open and supportive approach to all objections that might be brought up. Whether it be in person-to-person contact or in public presentations of a concept, the planner tries to involve everyone to create a groundwork of acceptance and understanding.

The problems of resistance can be approached with a crucial element, the power which comes from the authority the leader of the company has given. The space planner's power lies in the acceptance of his or her role by others. Early and exact definition of the planner and his or her role is a fundamental key to success.

The planner must command the respect of a company's leader in order to get this authority. Support of top management has a crucial effect on his or her ability to succeed. Designers must be able to communicate with the people who make decisions. Value judgments about design can only be made by top decision makers.

Most planners feel the most important person in the process is the president or chief executive officer. His or her involvement, understanding and leadership results in plans that are put into action. His or her actions get others involved. The president's own sense of commitment must be great and must be communicated to others. His or her involvement in the creative process is an invaluable asset, reinforcing the sense of purpose and involvement for everyone else.

chapter four
analysis
of the
organization

PLANNING FOR FLEXIBILITY

An organization is dynamic and changing. It is like a living organism — a living, breathing thing that expands and contracts. There are departments that will grow or shrink. There are business reverses or business booms and government controls that subject it to change. The organization must have flexibility to respond. Planning for flexibility is based on the data gathered, the inputs and outputs, their properties and relationships, and their restrictions and feedback controls. This constitutes the process which is the ongoing state of the planning system. The importance of having an ongoing system is the flexibility it affords the designer and management.

At AT&T, a recently created in-house staff of planners tries to keep up with change. Richard Bauer, chief space planner, described one of his problems, "The development of a new building is a very difficult thing to forecast from plan zero until we move in six years. We have to do our work, based on very tenuous forecasts. For example, the Marketing Department was formed a year ago. We talked to them about their growth potential and learned that they were just consolidating staff and had no plans for growth. It suddenly appeared that not only were they going to assimilate a couple of hundred people from other departments but they were also going to double in size. So, all of a sudden, we had a tremendous requirement for additional space on top of all the other departments' growth needs."

THE PLANNING SYSTEM

A systems approach to space planning is a method of handling the complex information gathered about the network of departments, the multitude of employees and the equipment they need. John Eberhard defines **systems** in two ways, as a noun and as a verb. When used as a noun, it describes a collection of objects and their interdependence. A system has to in-

Fig. 5. **Analysis and Critical Evaluation.**
(Courtesy Quickborner Team, Inc.)

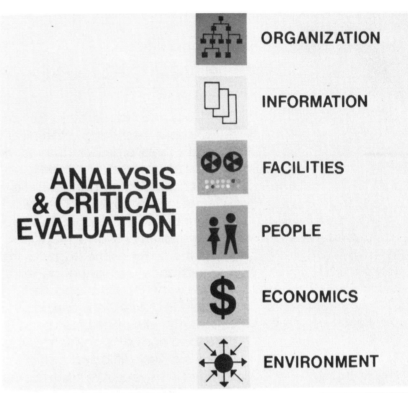

Fig. 6. **The dynamic flow of the planning process.**
(Courtesy Quickborner Team, Inc.)

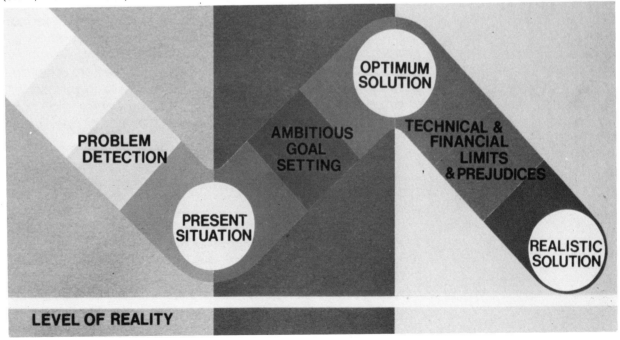

clude two or more components that are interdependent like an air-conditioning system or a partition system. When used as a verb, it describes a way of doing something to produce, through the process, a predicted result such as a planning system. Systems are concerned with describing reality in terms of analogies. Soft systems are words, hard systems are numbers. Systems analysis is the development of operations research which uses mathematical models. It involves analysis, synthesis, breaking down the information into small units and sub-groups to study the relationships between them (Fig. 5).

The planning system is complex. It consists of interconnected parts — office management systems, operational systems, office layout, tools, and people interacting with the building system to perform their work. That work is information gathering, decision-making, and communications. The designer's task is to create a high-performance work environment with the information gathered and measured against the performance goals set by the user.

The systems analysis procedure can be outlined very simply in six steps: (1) definition of the problem; (2) monitoring of the existing system in action; (3) analysis of the data collected to determine the requirements for a new system; (4) design of the new system, making use of available resources; (5) documentation of the new system and communication to those who will be affected by it; (6) implementation and long-term maintenance (Fig. 6).

The information can be coordinated horizontally or vertically. Information gathered this way can be codified, analyzed, and integrated by a computer. Data collection and computer use will be discussed in Chapters V and VI. Monitoring of the system in action provides the basis for planning by providing the intimate knowledge of how a company works. In Chapter III, the importance of close collaboration between the designer and the client was stressed. The client is a member of the planning team.

PRELIMINARY PLANNING

The orientation meeting is the beginning of every job. That is the top-level kickoff, where the company's key people meet the designers. It is an important meeting because it defines the role of the designer and provides the basis of the designer's authority. The designer's authority comes expressly from the chief executive officer and he or she must be present at the orientation meeting.

The orientation meeting is a chance to stimulate eager and enthusiastic discussion. The client is eager to talk about their feelings about their product, and how the planned changes will stimulate the company. They express what they feel the company is all about. It is the time to talk about design, its meaning to the company and their feelings about it. It is when the designer can express the function of design as part of the material aspects of the plan, interlocking and inseparable from the functional aspects of the work environment.

Another basic function of the orientation meeting is to establish the client's budget for the job. Budget must be discussed at this time, before planning. Most companies have earmarked funds for these changes. Their budgets and capital expenditures have been projected by their professional management. They know they can finance the projected changes. The orientation meeting will establish what the client's capabilities are. It is fundamental to planning to establish budget parameters. The client may be reluctant to become committed. A commitment at this time is very important to prevent misunderstanding and confusion as the work progresses.

Definition of the problem develops during the preplanning stages. Management will have set up a planning committee in earlier meetings with the planning consultant. The committee will articulate the goals and limitations they have set for themselves. They will provide detailed information about themselves to help acquaint the designer with the nature of the organization with which he or she is working. The designer learns about the organization and its plans for the future.

This readily available information is derived from organization charts, payroll personnel counts, and management studies. It may consist of the organizational structure and positions by title and department, personnel statistics, projections of growth by department or organizational changes, existing special facilities, and perhaps an inventory. Management may have had special studies done concerning their records management or word processing.

The basis for planning is the personnel requirements in relation to the standard work station. It forms the basis for 90 percent of the planning. The balance is made up of nonstandard items in the general office such as files, bookcases, work tables, or equipment that require space and proximity to specific people. Special office areas form the balance of space needs. These may be cafeterias, audiovisual rooms, conference areas, and so on.

THE VARIABLE FACTORS

Projected personnel requirements are the basis for planning. They depend on two variable factors. These factors are: (1) identifiable work units or groups, and (2) realistic planning periods.

Identifiable work groups, the building blocks of small units, provide information about a finite number of people. They form units of space needs that can be manipulated and moved around in the early planning stages. Some groups may have four people who work as a team, others may have ten, or twenty. You need such data because these are the groups that keep dropping out, popping up or growing in an organiztion (Fig. 7). This was illustrated by Richard Bauer's comments.

Information about realistic planning periods is based on what management knows about the present, the projected size of the organization when they move into the new facilities, and the maximum growth that must be accommodated. The first phase, the present, is where planning starts, with facts that are known. The second stage, the year of planned occupancy, is obviously important but is subsidiary to the third phase in time. The third phase is the real planning year — the year the company moves in, plus two years, or the life of the lease. Planning

this way is not based on finite numbers but on the range of possible changes in the future.

There are many factors over which management has so little control. They don't know what the regulating agencies or the government will allow. For example, will the Banking Commission allow branch banking outside the city, or through the state or world, or will the banks be able to run a travel business, or be in the insurance business? The future is based on the Banking Commissioner. Management has to have the capacity to respond (Figs. 8 and 9).

Management has to move in and survive the first lease, the first renewal period, or the first time they have an option to cancel or make a move. If they plan to move in next year with a five-year lease, planning must be set for six years. Management might plan to move in and slowly grow into other space that could be rented to another party. Theoretically, it can be done (the author does not know any successful instances of it). It is better to take the space and build in the expansion the company will need. It costs more and causes unbelievable disruption to expand after the company is in the space.

A classic example of such disruption and extra cost is shown by the First National City Bank. Twenty years ago they put up a $25 million building in New York. They've spent $50 million on interior renovation. Each time they tear down a wall they have to bring in every trade — carpenters, electricians, plumbers, air-conditioning service people, and the telephone company. The floors are tied up, nonproductively. People are moved about and work interrupted, adding immeasurably to the cost of the renovation work.

STANDARD AND NONSTANDARD CONDITIONS

Early planning is based on standard and nonstandard conditions. In the development of space requirements, the establishment of space standards is a basic step. Such standards are used to arrive at the overall space requirements. They are used repetitively. They establish area perimeters.

The use of standards formalized the space needs for repetitive

Opposite
Fig. 7. **The Port Authority is divided into a great number of departments and divisions whose activities change, enlarge, or diminish in time. They are distributed through twenty floors at the World Trade Center in New York City. One division may continue on several floors or as in other cases, several divisions may be located on a single floor. The changeable aspect of the open office system is ideal for this situation. There is no prevailing scheme for arranging the furniture components. Different groupings and arrangements have evolved around the functional relationship of the many departmental activities.**
(Courtesy Ford and Earl Design Associates)

Fig. 8. **One of the largest foreign-owned banking organizations in the United States, the J. Henry Schroder Banking Corporation, is a major tenant with a lease on nine floors of a building in New York City. To improve corporate function, they planned to utilize the ground floor by rearranging and consolidating adjacent functions. This corporate bank is exposed to the general public for the first time. Vacated space from the consolidation was subleased to help pay for expenditures on the new and renovated spaces.**
(Courtesy Ferguson Sorrentino Design Inc.)

Fig. 9. **The semi-flexible arrangement of seating and desks on the officer's platform of the J. Henry Schroder Banking Corporation provides a greater use of the space than a conventional arrangement and provides open conference areas for impromptu meetings. The flexible furniture system can be changed to add desks or replace seating as departmental needs demand. A mezzanine was constructed to accommodate the program and link the ground floor to the second floor.**
(Courtesy Ferguson Sorrentino Design Inc.)

Fig. 10. **Standards for mid-management offices at the Port Authority allow for effective functioning. They are furnished with oak desks and working conference areas. Within the open spaces there are many additional screened working conference areas, as well as at least one enclosed conference room on each floor containing complete display and projection facilities.**
(Courtesy Ford and Earl Design Associates)

38

Fig. 11. **Good sight lines as a result of raised floor levels in an audiovisual facility at Sears Roebuck and Company, Chicago.**
(Courtesy SLS Environetics)

Fig. 12. **Twin audiovisual facilities at the First National Bank of Chicago headquarters building.**
(Courtesy Ford and Earl Design Associates)

individual work functions and equipment. The amount of space needed in these standards should permit the most effective functioning of the personnel in that space and allow for modification and flexibility of furniture and function (Fig. 10). Work stations for all levels of personnel should be considered as square-foot areas, without determining specifics such as types of dividers or partitions, or furniture/partition systems. These options are considered at a later phase of design. People, multiplied by their work-station space standards, are the basis of all planning.

Special space requirements, or nonstandard conditions, are those that involve nonrepetitive or nonstandard equipment. Nonstandard equipment in the general office area are files,

Fig. 13. **Board room at the Trans America Corporation headquarters in San Francisco.**
(Courtesy Morganelli-Heumann Associates)

work tables, bookcases, and office machines that have space requirements and require proximity to specific people. Specialized facilities have individual requirements that are based on functional needs rather than on personnel count. They may be repetitive, such as several conference rooms, or unique. The individual requirements for these special rooms must be studied separately. A small sketch should accompany the presentation of this type of information to further illustrate the special conditions.

Nonstandard facilities are the most challenging to design and are the most expensive part of the plan. They might require additional needs like smoke exhaust in conference areas, special circuits, raised floors, special acoustic treatment, or audiovisual requirements (Figs. 11, 12, and 13). To help management evaluate what they are asking for it is good to compare it to what they have. These facilities are always custom installations requiring special architectural features as well as special equipment or security. Herbert Newmark, an independent consultant, formerly with H. M. Keiser collects this information in two parallel lists: the present special facility with its basic capacity and the required new facility with its capacity. For example, if a reception area presently seats four, it may be required to seat six. A library that presently has 1,000 books will need 12,000 books in the future. He feels that this method of collecting special requirements is useful to management in evaluating costly custom facilities.

MAXIMUM AND MINIMUM CONDITIONS

The range of the future, discussed earlier in this chapter in the section on variable factors, encompasses what a company's maximum and minimum conditions might be over the next ten years. The maximum will indicate how much growth should be planned for, how much space should be leased or how much should be held under option. The minimum will indicate how much the company must be prepared to pare down its operations if it were forced to reduce itself to its minimum. The concept of expansion and contraction is important because of its influence on planning and the location of the special facilities. So much of the budget will be allocated on special facilities that if contraction is necessary it must be planned that they remain in the active functioning areas. If contraction is necessary and space must be sublet, special areas should not be isolated and departments should not be split. In planning, it is advisable to plan for the worst situation. Include in the plan every special condition that is needed for the present plus six months, but be prepared to cut down.

To get rid of excess space and not impair the functioning of the company will mean consolidating all the special facilities in the space that is the hard core of the company. In a company of 600 people, 400 people might represent the hard core, which might mean four floors. This is typical in a 20,000 square-foot floor with 100 people per floor. Those four floors should include everything that cannot be rented to others and that costs so much to have custom built, such as the cafeteria, the board room, the fancy executive offices, the mailroom, or heavy print shop. Companies find that when they sublease a floor in the middle, that can create serious problems such as split departments or impaired use of elevators.

THE PRELIMINARY REPORT

The preliminary report is an analysis of the company presenting the material that has been discussed. The preliminary report examines management's requirements, the space standards, and special facilities. The report projects them over a range of possible changes in the future. This material is posted on summary sheets. It represents a picture of a fluid situation over a time period. It is not a space analysis but an analysis of the company's needs. Management must review this report and agree with its analysis.

The report may be presented to top management or members of top management and the facilities planning committee. This committee and a planning coordinator represent the company in their dealings with the space planner. The committee may be made up of representatives from the president or director and from the comptroller and other departments concerned with the planning of the organization. They give authority to the person selected as the planning coordinator. They articulate the goals of the company and establish schedules, set limits to budget and space demands, and establish review and approval procedures.

The committee reviews all the data. It can request special studies to be made to supplement and assist the planner. Studies made by special consultants outside the company are respected and management often listens to their recommendations. Studies such as those on record management and paper flow systems, word processing systems, and real estate studies are possibilities.

If the planning committee has been working closely with the space planner, the preliminary report may also include initial space analysis and a tentative budget projection. When the basic personnel requirements are established determining work-station standards, space studies based on these standards can be developed. Projection of space needs can be calculated from the number of personnel and their work-station standards, space studies based on these standards can be developed. Projection of space needs can be calculated from the number of personnel and their work-station areas, plus the space requirements of the special facilities.

chapter five
data
collection

INTERVIEWING

The cornerstone of space planning is data collection. It provides the factual information in numbers and the verbal description for analysis and design.

Data collection starts right from the beginning. The orientation meeting with the client is the first step. This initial meeting is like a group encounter with everyone eager to contribute. As mentioned in Chapter IV, the orientation meeting involves the top executives, and explores management goals, the corporate identity, and how design can give it expression. The meeting also establishes certain limits of time and budget.

The orientation meeting will yield readily available information as well. The company can produce statistics on its past growth and its present organization structure. It can supply statistics on personnel by departments and titles as well as projected organization changes and growth plans. The designer is now ready to involve and ask questions of the larger body of employees.

People from the design firm, who are trained to do the interviews, are introduced to the company by someone appointed to act as a liaison or guide. The guide may be an office manager or an executive. If it is an executive, it may be one of two types. One type of executive might be a bright young person who will learn about the organization as the designer does. The other executive choice might be one who is planning to retire and who does not want ongoing responsibilities. This role gives the older executive a special function. This executive is the ideal guide because he is aware of what is going on in the company, knows the history of events, and how to answer questions. He also knows where the bodies are buried.

Jack Dunbar, who said there was no substitute for finding out how a particular company worked except by moving in and directly observing "down to the last paper cup," says that time is a basic consideration. The amount of time required for data collection is directly related to the amount of information gathered.

One aspect in evaluating the client's needs is the importance of giving attention to the opinions of employees during data

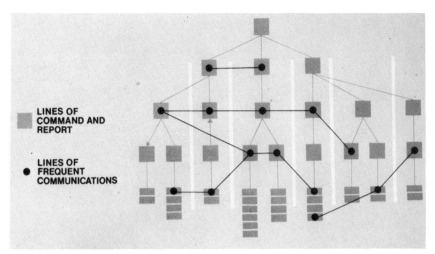

LINES OF
COMMAND AND
REPORT

LINES OF
FREQUENT
COMMUNICATIONS

Fig. 14. **The relationship of the formal organization and the lines of communication within it are shown. The typical formal hierarchy does not reflect the communications interaction.**
(Courtesy Quickborner Team, Inc.)

collection interviews. The people who are consulted feel involved in the results. The consideration given to their feelings predisposes them to accept the results of the planning.

People trained to do interviews have discovered something about the professional listener. The professional listener is generally assumed to be a sympathizer. This person has come to hear your thoughts and your thoughts are considered to be significant and worthy. This gives the person a feeling of confidence. Information is obtained easily. Problems are brought out more readily.

Some design firms collect data or interview every person employed by the company. Other designers establish with management who is to be interviewed because management will want some people included for political purposes. Corporate hierarchy sometimes dictates who is interviewed but, frequently, the people who have the needed information are the people who control special areas, even though they are outside the hierarchy (Fig. 14).

The material collected during the interviews is entered onto forms and reviewed several times with management. This verification is very important as it corrects errors in judgment, duplications, and misinformation. It also serves to call attention to information of which management might not have been aware Such information usually surfaces as the result of the interviews.

REQUIRED INFORMATION

What information is needed? Basically, the interviewer gathers information that can quantify and describe what is required for work flow, equipment, and special facilities. The interviewer will gather and detail the following specifics:

1. Work flow. How do people work in the organization? How do they work together, and how many workers are there?

2. Work function. What tasks are performed? How are they classified in the organization hierarchy? Are there privacy requirements? What special equipment is required for the work function? What are the individual work-station requirements?

3. Communication within the department. What are the personnel relationships and priorities relevant to the work flow (Fig. 15)?

4. Communication between departments. What are the interdepartmental contacts, their frequency of communication and their need for shared facilities? Is the contact made in person, by telephone, or in writing?

5. Communication with the public. What is the frequency and nature of the contact? How great a penetration and interaction is there with personnel? Are special facilities or services needed for this contact such as waiting rooms, dining facilities, or auditoriums (Fig. 16)?

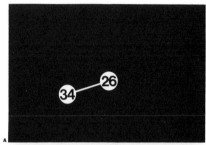

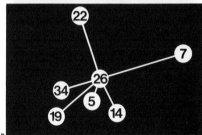

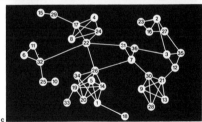

Fig. 15. **Communications analysis starts with a study of an individual's communications patterns (A), which is expanded into task-related groups (B), and then to larger groups or departments (C).**
(Courtesy Herman Miller Inc.)

Fig. 16. **Special facilities and services needed for contact with the public includes easily understood graphics.**
(Courtesy Ford and Earl Design Associates)

Fig. 17. **The cafeteria at the Weyerhaeuser Company headquarters in Tacoma seats 350 people. While most executives eat here, another dining room is reserved for special luncheon meetings and visitors. The red flocked ceiling and the grid of glittering lights give the large room warmth and excitement.**
(Courtesy Skidmore, Owings and Merrill)

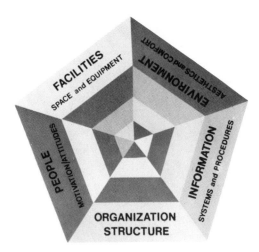

Fig. 18. **The basic data that describes an organization can yield information about space needs and the budget.**
(Courtesy The Quickborner Team, Inc.)

6. Communication and information relevant to paper flow. What are the requirements for clerical services, typing pools, and word processing centers? How are documents distributed?

7. Record storage. What type of record storage is needed? What is used for active work, what are the quantities and types of storage units, both active and inactive? Where should they be located and what facilities can be shared?

8. Special facilities. What are they and how do they function? How many people do they accommodate? What special requirements do they need, both structural and functional? What furniture and equipment is needed for areas like mailrooms, conference rooms, lounges and libraries (Fig. 17)?

9. Special equipment. What is required? Who uses it? What are its structural and functional requirements for floor space, wiring, or support? What are the structural and functional requirements needed for items like vaults, computers, food service, projection equipment, and communications systems?

10. Existing equipment. An inventory of equipment and its condition for re-use is noted.

FROM DATA TO DESIGN

The information gathered, reviewed, revised, and approved by management provides a basic body of knowledge that describes the organization. It is then analyzed by getting personnel counts, studying relationship priorities, and developing a set of space standards for both work stations and special facilities. It is also presented as a preliminary report. The data can then be used two ways at once, to yield space as well as budget information (Fig. 18). The designer is now a position to tell the client the three things the client wants to know — how much space will be needed, what the design concept is, and what it will cost in furniture and equipment. This is the result of the constraints and goals established at the orientation meeting.

The space needs are arrived at from the space standards established for the work stations and special facilities. They are used to establish area perimeters for the overall requirements accommodating the needs of personnel and departments. The space standards will reflect the design concept as well as the functional needs.

For example, if a designer has decided to use open, unbroken spaces in the office, he or she might decide that large spaces between people are needed to achieve verbal privacy. That would entail a larger space standard than a design concept using small private offices.

How does the designer arrive at the design concept and the space requirements? That is "the art part" of space planning. The art of space planning represents the unique contribution of the designer. Many design firms can take the collected data and arrive at similar space and budget solutions, but that does not minimize their creative contribution to the solution or detract from the design firm that has arrived at a different solution. The design concept is what influences the final decision and evaluation. It will reflect how well the designer understood and translated the client's needs and incorporated the intangible, "the art part," into the design. It is a measure of a design's success that its aesthetic, functional, and material aspects are so utterly fused that they cannot be isolated easily.

METHODS AND FORMS

There are several methods of gathering information such as using questionnaires, interviewing, and observing. Every design firm develops its own techniques. Its forms and questionnaires are sometimes guarded zealously. After all, the forms and questionnaires represent the way the firm does its business. This represents an investment in thought and analysis of the problems of effective data collection. It is understandable from that point of view that many firms have a desire for exclusivity of information-gathering techniques.

Questionnaires have been developed that yield **quantitative** data and are easy to analyze. They can be administered to large or small groups and so they are efficient in time and effort. Individual interviews, by contrast, are more time consuming and yield **qualitative** information that takes longer to analyze, but many people respond better to the conversational manner of an interview. By combining an interview with a previously submitted questionnaire, a great deal of information can be obtained. In addition, most designers feel that there is no substitute for going to the organization and observing everyone at their tasks.

Using questionnaires to discover an organization's functional and physical needs provides basic facts and figures. The Herman Miller Company has developed a two-part survey that they administer to every employee in an organization. They are able to completely administer both forms to a given group in the space of one hour. The size of the group is basically determined by the space available and the work schedule of the organization. Normally group sizes run approximately from twenty-five to forty people. They have on occasion taken larger groups in excess of 100 when the space allowed. Through the use of these forms Herman Miller can illicit a response from a large number of people in relatively little time; certainly less time than it would take to individually interview each person.

The computer program which develops the output reports from the information collected by these forms does so in very little time. The material is presented in a form that the Herman Miller planners can immediately put to use. The time-consuming task of interpreting the individual's responses into a working document is virtually eliminated. Since Herman Miller actually administers the forms to every employee involved in the project, they obtain a broad-based response.

The two forms, an activity equipment analysis (Table 4) and a communication interaction analysis (Table 5), are reproduced here. They are excellent examples of questionnaires designed to get quantitative empirical data and to obtain the information quickly.

The forms yield information that Herman Miller uses as the basis for several reports. One report provides a general description of the work surface, filing, storage, display, communications, and seating requirements of each person surveyed. This is used to develop individual equipment specifications and to determine preliminary budgets and equipment standards programs. Another report deals with individual interaction that is used as the basis for developing the major communications groups that exist within the organization. This can be represent-

Table 4. **ACTIVITY EQUIPMENT ANALYSIS**
(Courtesy Herman Miller Design Resource Service)

Instructions: The questions on the following pages should be answered by circling the number next to the answer which most nearly agrees with your activities.

Work Surface

1. During an average work week, how many hours do you spend reading hard bound volumes, computer printouts, periodicals, letters, memos, etc.?
   - 1-5 hours — 1
   - 5-10 hours — 2
   - 10-15 hours — 3
   - 15-20 hours — 4
   - Over 20 hours — 5

2. During an average work week how many hours do you spend writing or dictating letters, memos, reports, computer programs, etc.?
   - 1-5 hours — 1
   - 5-10 hours — 2
   - 10-15 hours — 3
   - 15-20 hours — 4
   - Over 20 hours — 5

3. During an average work week how many hours do you spend doing bookkeeping, order entry, filing or similar activities?
   - 1-5 hours — 1
   - 5-10 hours — 2
   - 10-15 hours — 3
   - 15-20 hours — 4
   - Over 20 hours — 5

4. How frequently does your job require you to have books, manuals, ledgers or other reference materials spread out in your work area while working on your normal job tasks?
   - Never — 1
   - Infrequently — 2
   - Sometimes — 3
   - Frequently — 4
   - Very Frequently — 5

5. How frequently does your job require you to work with computer printouts?
   - Never — 1
   - Infrequently — 2
   - Sometimes — 3
   - Frequently — 4
   - Very Frequently — 5

6. How frequently do you refer to large drawings, maps, charts, etc., while working on your normal job tasks?
   - Never — 1
   - Infrequently — 2
   - Sometimes — 3
   - Frequently — 4
   - Very Frequently — 5

7. How frequently are large drawings, maps, charts, etc., spread out during conferences or meetings in your work space?
   - Never — 1
   - Infrequently — 2
   - Sometimes — 3
   - Frequently — 4
   - Very Frequently — 5

8. Which, if any, of the following machines does your job require you to operate?
   - Calculator — 1
   - Typewriter — 2
   - Mag Card or Mag Tape — 3
   - Keypunch — 4
   - Computer Terminal — 5
   - Microfilm/Fiche Reader — 6
   - Telex — 7
   - None — 8

If your answer to this question was "None", go to question 11; otherwise, continue with the next question.

9. Which, if any, of the machines mentioned in question 8 do you share with any of your co-workers?
   - Calculator — 1
   - Typewriter — 2
   - Mag Card or Mag Tape — 3
   - Keypunch — 4
   - Computer Terminal — 5
   - Microfilm/Fiche Reader — 6
   - Telex — 7
   - None — 8

10. If you have a calculator, please indicate the type.
    - Mechanical — 1
    - Electronic — 2

11. During an average work week how many hours do you spend sorting or collating papers for distribution or filing?
    - 1-5 hours — 1
    - 5-10 hours — 2
    - 10-15 hours — 3
    - 15-20 hours — 4
    - Over 20 hours — 5

12. During an average work week how many hours do you spend drawing, drafting or preparing large graphic materials?
    - 1-5 hours — 1
    - 5-10 hours — 2
    - 10-15 hours — 3
    - 15-20 hours — 4
    - Over 20 hours — 5

13. During an average work week how many conferences or meetings do you participate in?
    - None — 1
    - 1-5 — 2
    - 5-10 — 3
    - 10-15 — 4
    - More than 15 — 5

If your answer to this question was "None", go to question 17; otherwise, continue with the next question.

14. Where are your conferences most frequently held?
    - Own work space or office — 1
    - Private conference room — 2
    - Someone else's work space — 3
    - No pattern — 4

15. On an average, how long do these conferences last?
    - Less than 10 minutes — 1
    - 10-30 minutes — 2
    - 30 minutes to 1 hour — 3
    - 1-2 hours — 4
    - Over 2 hours — 5

16. Not including yourself, how many other persons usually participate in these conferences?
    - 1-2 persons — 1
    - 2-3 persons — 2
    - 3-4 persons — 3
    - 4-5 persons — 4
    - More than 5 persons — 5

17. In completing your daily work tasks, what is your preferred work posture?
    - Sitting — 1
    - Standing — 2
    - Sitting and Standing — 3
    - No preference — 4

Filing

18. Do you have and/or maintain any files in a central or departmental file area?
    - Yes — 1
    - No — 2

51

Table 4 (con't.)

If your answer to this question was "No", go to question 33; if "Yes", continue with the next question.

When answering the questions in the remainder of this section, please consider only those files that you have and/or maintain in your own work space.

20 Are any of these files located in desk or credenza drawers such as:

- Yes — 1
- No — 2

If your answer to this question was "No", go to question 23; if "Yes", continue with the next question.

21 How many of these desk or credenza drawers are filled with working files, i.e., information which is referred to periodically throughout the day?

- 1 drawer or less — 1
- 2 drawers — 2
- 3 drawers — 3
- 4 drawers — 4
- More than 4 drawers — 5

22 How many of these drawers contain legal size material?

- None — 1
- 1 drawer or less — 2
- 2 drawers — 3
- 3 drawers — 4
- 4 drawers or more — 5

23 Are any of these files contained within standard filing cabinets such as:

- Yes — 1
- No — 2

If your answer to this question was "No", go to question 26; if "Yes", continue with the next question.

24 How many of these standard file drawers are filled with working files, i.e., information which is referred to periodically throughout the day?

- 1 drawer or less — 1
- 2 drawers — 2
- 3 drawers — 3
- 4 drawers — 4
- 5 drawers — 5
- More than 5 drawers — 6

25 How many of these drawers contain legal size material?

- None — 1
- 1 drawer or less — 2
- 2 drawers — 3
- 3 drawers — 4
- 4 drawers — 5
- 5 drawers or more — 6

26 Are any of these files contained within lateral filing cabinets such as:

- Yes — 1
- No — 2

If your answer to this question was "No", go to question 29; if "Yes", continue with the next question.

27 How many of these lateral files are filled with working files, i.e., information which is referred to periodically throughout the day?

- 1 drawer or less — 1
- 2 drawers — 2
- 3 drawers — 3
- 4 drawers — 4
- 5 drawers — 5
- More than 5 drawers — 6

28 How many of these drawers contain legal size material?

- None — 1
- 1 drawer or less — 2
- 2 drawers — 3
- 3 drawers — 4
- 4 drawers — 5
- 5 drawers or more — 6

29 Do any of the files you maintain contain dead files, i.e., information which must be kept but which is seldom retrieved?

- Yes — 1
- No — 2

30 Do you have a need for any special size filing cabinets such as EDP, card, etc. in your work area?

- Yes — 1
- No — 2

31 Do you share working files with any of your co-workers and need file storage that can be easily moved from one work space to another?

- Yes — 1
- No — 2

32 How adequate is the amount of filing you currently use?

- Very adequate — 1
- Somewhat adequate — 2
- Adequate — 3
- Somewhat inadequate — 4
- Very inadequate — 5

Storage

33 Do you store computer printouts or punch cards in your work space?

- Yes — 1
- No — 2

Table 4 (con't.)

If your answer to this question was "No", go to question 36; if "Yes", continue with the next question.

34 If the computer printouts needed in your work space were stacked, how high would the pile be?

None	1
1 foot or less	2
4-5 feet	3
6-7 feet	4
More than 7 feet	5

35 How many punch cards do you need in your work space?

None	1
3 boxes or less	2
4-10 boxes	3
10-15 boxes	4
15-20 boxes	5
20-30 boxes	6
More than 30 boxes	7

36 Excluding computer printouts, how many lineal feet of books, periodicals, notebooks, folders, etc. less than 1" thick do you need in your work space?

Less than 2 feet	1
2-4 feet	2
4-6 feet	3
6-8 feet	4
More than 8 feet	5

37 Excluding computer printouts, how many lineal feet of catalogs, books, manuals, binders, etc. from 1" to 3" thick do you need in your work space?

Less than 2 feet	1
2-4 feet	2
4-6 feet	3
6-8 feet	4
More than 8 feet	5

38 Excluding computer printouts, how many lineal feet of catalogs, binders, manuals, books, etc., over 3" thick do you need in your work space?

Less than 2 feet	1
2-4 feet	2
4-6 feet	3
6-8 feet	4
More than 8 feet	5

39 Is any of your reference material contained in a map case or plan file such as:

Yes	1
No	2

40 Do you store stationery, business forms, slides, samples, or other miscellaneous items in your work space?

Yes	1
No	2

41 If the miscellaneous items mentioned in question 40 were taken from your work space, how many 4 foot long shelves would they fill?

1 shelf or less	1
2 shelves	2
3 shelves	3
4 shelves	4
More than 4 shelves	5

42 How many of the shelves mentioned in question 41 should be deeper than 12 inches?

None	1
1 shelf	2
2 shelves	3
3 shelves	4
4 shelves or more	5

Display

43 How frequently do you have large graphic materials such as flow charts, maps, pert charts, etc. on display?

Never	1
Infrequently	2
Sometimes	3
Frequently	4
Very Frequently	5

44 How frequently do you display current periodicals or project folders as reminders or triggers for your work activity?

Never	1
Infrequently	2
Sometimes	3
Frequently	4
Very Frequently	5

45 While working or in conferences, how frequently do you use an easel? If you do not have an easel, how frequently would it be useful?

Never	1
Infrequently	2
Sometimes	3
Frequently	4
Very Frequently	5

46 While working or in conferences, how frequently do you write or draw on a chalkboard? If you do not have a chalkboard, how frequently would it be useful?

Never	1
Infrequently	2
Sometimes	3
Frequently	4
Very Frequently	5

Communications

47 How many telephone calls do you place or receive during an average day?

1-10	1
10-20	2
20-30	3
30-40	4
Over 40	5

48 What portion of your telephone calls must be kept confidential from your fellow employees?

None	1
1-25%	2
25-50%	3
50-75%	4
Over 75%	5

49 Do you personally have any dictating equipment such as a dictaphone, PBX, etc.?

Yes	1
No	2

50 Besides a dictaphone or telephone do you have any other communications equipment on your work surface such as a speakerphone, intercom, etc.?

Yes	1
No	2

51 During an average work day, how many copies will you personally make on a copy machine?

None	1
1-25	2
25-50	3
Over 50	4

Table 5. **COMMUNICATIONS**
INTERACTION ANALYSIS
(Courtesy Herman Miller Design Resource Service)

Instructions: Print your name and department in the spaces provided.

Please consider those individuals with whom you work most closely and print their names in the spaces marked "co-worker". **Place only one person's name in each space.** The individuals whom you cite need not be in the same department or on the same corporate level that you are. The only prerequisite is that they must also be participating in the survey. If there is doubt, it is best to include them.

Answer each of the following questions for each of these individuals. **Choose only one answer for each question.** Indicate your choice by circling the appropriate letter on the answer sheet. Additional answer sheets will be supplied if needed.

e x a m p l e

Andrew H. Hayworth
name (first/middle initial/last)

Accounting
department

	John Mills co-worker	_Linda Smith_ co-worker	_Cyndi Brown_ co-worker	co-worker	_Tom Wellesly_ co-worker
1	A (B) C D E	A B (C) D E	A (B) C D E	A B C D (E)	A B C D (E)

1 Do you receive new information from this individual which may eventually be applied to your area of responsibility?
A Almost always   B Often   C No established pattern   D Seldom   E Almost never

name (first/middle initial/last)

department

	co-worker	co-worker	co-worker	co-worker	co-worker
1	A B C D E	A B C D E	A B C D E	A B C D E	A B C D E
2	A B C D E	A B C D E	A B C D E	A B C D E	A B C D E
3	A B C D E	A B C D E	A B C D E	A B C D E	A B C D E
4	A B C D E	A B C D E	A B C D E	A B C D E	A B C D E
5	A B C D E	A B C D E	A B C D E	A B C D E	A B C D E
6	A B C D E	A B C D E	A B C D E	A B C D E	A B C D E
7	A B C D E	A B C D E	A B C D E	A B C D E	A B C D E
8	A B C D E	A B C D E	A B C D E	A B C D E	A B C D E
9	A B C D E	A B C D E	A B C D E	A B C D E	A B C D E
10	A B C D E	A B C D E	A B C D E	A B C D E	A B C D E
11	A B C D E	A B C D E	A B C D E	A B C D E	A B C D E
12	A B C D E	A B C D E	A B C D E	A B C D E	A B C D E
13	A B C D E	A B C D E	A B C D E	A B C D E	A B C D E
14	A B C D E	A B C D E	A B C D E	A B C D E	A B C D E

1 Do you receive new information from this individual which may eventually be applied to your area of responsibility?
A Almost always   B Often   C No established pattern   D Seldom   E Almost never

2 Does this individual guide the conduct of your routine office activity?
A Almost always   B Often   C No established pattern   D Seldom   E Almost never

3 Does the information received from this individual provide you with alternative approaches and/or solutions to your particular task?
A Almost always   B Often   C No established pattern   D Seldom   E Almost never

4 Do you retain the information received from this individual for future reference?
A Almost always   B Often   C No established pattern   D Seldom   E Almost never

5 Does the information supplied by this individual outline the methods or procedures which you follow when performing your task?
A Almost always   B Often   C No established pattern   D Seldom   E Almost never

6 Would you seek an opinion from this individual even though it may challenge your decision regarding a specific subject?
A Almost always   B Often   C No established pattern   D Seldom   E Almost never

7 Do you discuss general ideas or concepts with this individual which pertain to your work activity?
A Almost always   B Often   C No established pattern   D Seldom   E Almost never

8 Do you receive announcements or directives from this individual which concern the total organizational activity?
A Almost always   B Often   C No established pattern   D Seldom   E Almost never

9 Do you confer with this individual on topics relative to your particular task prior to taking action on them?
A Almost always   B Often   C No established pattern   D Seldom   E Almost never

10 Do you supply this individual with general information which applies to his/her area of responsibility?
A Almost always   B Often   C No established pattern   D Seldom   E Almost never

11 Do you direct the course of this individual's administrative activity?
A Almost always   B Often   C No established pattern   D Seldom   E Almost never

12 Do you advise this individual concerning decisions which he/she must make?
A Almost always   B Often   C No established pattern   D Seldom   E Almost never

13 How would you rate the importance of communication contact with this individual in terms of your activity?
A Very great   B Great   C Some   D Little   E Very little

14 How frequently do you communicate with this individual when performing your task activity?
A Continually throughout the day   B Several times per day   C Several times per week   D Several times per month   E Several times per year

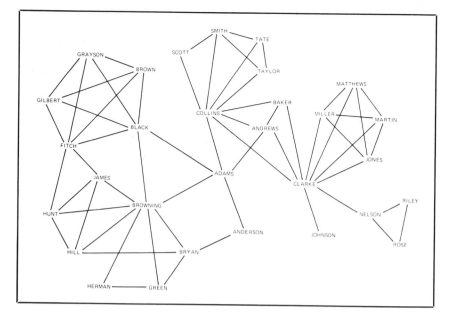

Fig. 19. **Individual interaction diagram.**
(Courtesy Herman Miller Inc.)

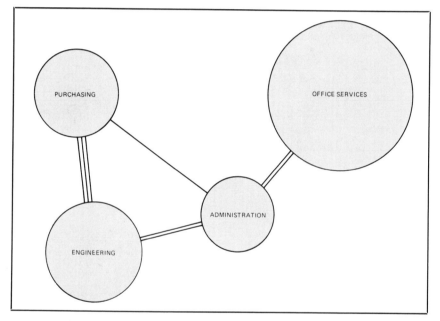

Fig. 20. **Departmental interaction diagram.**
(Courtesy Herman Miller Inc.)

ed diagrammatically in an individual interaction diagram (Fig. 19). The information can also be read in terms of inter- and intra-departmental links that exist within the organization (Fig. 20). The internal links are compiled for each department first and then are followed by a listing of external links. This can be represented graphically in a departmental interaction diagram.

In contrast, S.L.S. Environetics utilizes a departmental interview questionnaire (Table 6). It is designed to get much the same information and some additional information as well. Since the forms are filled out by someone representing a department head, the survey covers more qualitative responses and also reveals company plans such as the anticipated purchase of new equipment or large scale changes that may be contemplated for the department. It does not provide for a detailed

departmental interview questionnaire

Date _____ Company _____
Department _____ Department Head _____
Present Location: Building _____ Floor _____
Person Interviewed _____ Title _____

1. Please supply an organization chart of your department.
2. Please supply a listing of present approved positions.

3. What is the general function of your department? _____
_____
_____
_____
_____

4. Is your department now in two or more geographic locations? _____

Unit	Location

5. Which units of your department should be located near each other for best operation?

Unit	Located Near

6. With what other departments do you work closely?

Department	Type of Contact

7. What records do you store?

		Number of Storage Units		
Type of Record	Type of Storage	Present	Annual Growth	Retired Annually

Describe any contemplated changes in your record storage.
_____
_____
_____

8. Do you have a separate data processing installation in your department?
Yes _____ No _____
What configuration of electronic data processing equipment is planned for the future?
_____
_____
_____
_____

9. What type of equipment (other than typewriters or adding machines) do you now use?
_____
_____
_____

10. Do you use any other special equipment requiring floor space? Please describe.

Type of Equipment	Number of Units	Comments

Do you anticipate the purchase of any new equipment? Please describe.

_____
_____
_____
_____
_____

11. Please describe the need for conference facilities within your department.

Type of Meeting	Number of People	Frequency of Meeting

12. Do you use a secretarial pool, shared secretaries, private secretaries or a combination of these?

_____
_____
_____
_____

13. How many people have to be seated at one time in a reception area for your department?

_____
_____
_____
_____

14. Are there any large scale changes contemplated for your Department?

_____
_____
_____
_____

15. What are the major shortcomings in the type of space presently available to your Department?

_____
_____
_____
_____

16. Please list the number and type of positions in your department. (Show by department number any position located in your space, but assigned to another department).

	Position Title	Type of Space*		Number of Positions		
		Present	Future	Present Authorized	1978	1983
	Total					

*Legend for type of space

PO	Private Office	BSO	Bank Screen Office (5'-0" partition)
1/2 PO	Person Private Office	1/2 BSO	2 Person Bank Screen Office
1/3 PO	3 Person Private Office	1/3 BSO	3 Person Bank Screen Office
OA	Open Area		

Component _____ Page _____

SLS special observations.

_____
_____
_____
_____
_____

1 ASSOCIATED SPACE DESIGN, INC.
44 Broad Street, N.W.
Atlanta, Georgia 30303

Completed by:	Section	Department:	Division:
Title:	Section Head:	Dep't. Head:	Div. Head:
Date completed:	Date reviewed:	Date reviewed:	Date reviewed:

PERSONNEL			SPACE						EQUIPMENT													SPECIAL AREA	
			Sex	Loca-tion	Type		Mtgs.	Phone					Priv. files			Priv. Shel.		Group Files			Group Shel.		
Number	Name	Job Title and Function	Male / Female	Bldg. / Floor	Private Office / Semi-Private / Open	No. per Day / Avg. No. Present		Private Tel. / Share Tel.	Furniture	No. Guest Chairs.	Elect. Equip. and Business Machines	Noisy Mach. Oper.	No. of Cab.	Drwrs. per cab.	Type of File	Open (lin. ft.)	Closed (lin. ft.)	No. of Cab.	Drwrs. per Cab.	Type of File	Open (lin. ft.)	Closed (lin. ft.)	Name and/or Description of Area	Approx. Size
	a	b	c	d	e	f	g	h	i	j	k		l	m	n	o	p	q	r	s	t	u	v	w	x

Table 7. **FACILITIES REQUIREMENT ANALYSIS**
(Courtesy Associated Space Design Incorporated)

analysis of equipment by the user but it is accompanied by an inventory sheet (Table 8). Since the questionnaire is also accompanied by an interview, additional information is developed.

Another example of a questionnaire is one provided by Associated Space Design Incorporated (Table 7). Their space requirements analysis was formulated over ten years ago but has had basic revisions. The forms are constantly reviewed and adjusted for specific projects. After the forms have been completed and reviewed, clarifications, amplifications, and qualitative information are obtained by interviews.

The forms are distributed to key personnel and are designed to provide the basic facts and figures as well as special requirements such as lighting or plumbing fixtures and special problems such as noise. The forms also ask the important questions of anticipated growth or reduction of departments.

In light of the proprietary interest design firms have in their data-collecting material, these three companies are making a valuable and substantive contribution. They have taken the attitude of other professional groups such as medicine or law of sharing vital information for the good of the profession as a whole and for the benefit of the clients.

2 PRESENT SPACE

Is your floor area and location adequate for present needs?   Yes   No   If not, why?

a. General crowded conditions.   Yes   No

b. Lack of privacy for key personnel.   Yes   No   If yes, is lack of privacy primarily visual _____, acoustical _____, security _____?

c. Lack of storage for *actively* used material.   Yes   No

d. Interference by through traffic from other departments.   Yes   No

e. Poor location in relation to other departments.   Yes   No

f. Inefficient layout of floor space.   Yes   No

3 FUTURE PERSONNEL REQUIREMENTS

Estimate *only* the additions or reductions in personnel during the periods shown, *not* the cumulative total employees required during those periods. Describe new job functions.

Title Job Function	Present to 12-31-76	12-31-76 to 12-31-78	12-31-78 to 12-31-80	12-31-80 to 12-31-85
Totals				

Comments about present space.

_____
_____
_____
_____
_____

4 INTERACTION WITH OTHER SECTIONS OR DEPARTMENTS

a. With what sections in your department or other departments does your section communicate most?

Within your department   With other departments

1. _____   1. _____
2. _____   2. _____
3. _____   3. _____
4. _____   4. _____

Comments _____
_____
_____
_____

b. Describe special conditions or requirements regarding circulation *within* your group.

_____
_____
_____

5 ANTICIPATED FILE GROWTH (Total no. of *drawers,* not cabinets.)

Estimate *only* additions or reductions in files during periods shown, not the cumulative total files required during those periods. This is for group files, not private files.

Type of File	Present to 12-31-76	12-31-76 to 12-31-78	12-31-78 to 12-31-80	12-31-80 to 12-31-85
Letter Size				
Legal Size				
Card Files				
Keypunch Card				
Comp. Printout				
Microfilm				

6 EXPANSION Please provide any additional comments pertinent to expected expansion. _____

_____
_____
_____
_____
_____

7 SPECIAL CONDITIONS If your group will require any of the following special elements, please describe the specific functions for which they are required.

a. Lighting _____
b. Electrical Power Supply _____
c. Heating or Cooling _____
d. Acoustical Treatment _____
e. Plumbing other than standard restroom facilities _____

8 CONFERENCE AREAS If conference space for your group is required, other than at work stations, please indicate below:

a. No. of conferences per week _____
b. Avg. no. of persons present _____
c. Max. no. of persons present _____
d. Average length of conference _____ hour(s)
e. No. of hours per week used _____
f. Special equipment required: _____
   Chalkboard _____, Tackboard _____, Clock _____, Display rail _____, Projection _____, Other _____
g. Storage and other requirements (describe) _____

9 MECHANIZATION If additional mechanization of office processes is anticipated within the near future, describe specifically. _____

_____
_____

10 COMMENTS If there are other conditions peculiar to your group, or you have additional comments or recommendations that might be beneficial, attach supplementary material.

Table 7 (con't.)

PERSONNEL			EXISTING									PROPOSED			
			EXISTING SPACE	EQUIPMENT							PTG. REQ.	SPACE	EQUIPMENT		PTG. REQ.
NO.	TITLE	NAME		QTY.	ITEM	SIZE IN INCHES						TYPE	LOC. NEAR	QTY.	ITEM
						W	D	M	CON						

SECTION

LEGEND

TYPE OF SPACE		**DESKS**		**FILES**	
PO	PRIVATE OFFICE	DP	DOUBLE PEDESTAL	4 DR. LET	4 DRAWER LETTER FILE
½ PO	2 PERSON PRIVATE OFFICE	SP (L or R)	SINGLE PEDESTAL (LEFT or RIGHT)	4 DR. LEG	4 DRAWER LEGAL FILE
BSO	BANK SCREEN OFFICE	ST (L or R)	SECRETARIAL TYPING (LEFT or RIGHT)	BC	BOOKCASE
½ BSO	2 PERSON BANK SCREEN OFFICE				
OA	OPEN AREA	**CHAIRS**		**TABLES**	
		ES	EXECUTIVE SWIVEL	T	TABLE
		P	POSTURE	TT	TYPING TABLE
		SWA	SIDE CHAIR WITH ARMS		
		S	SIDE CHAIR WITHOUT ARMS	**CONDITION**	
				N	NEW
				G	GOOD
				P	POOR

Table 8. **INVENTORY FORM**

(Courtesy SLS Environetics)

chapter six
using
the
computer

THE GOLDEN PENCIL

Designers and architects work, for the most part, within small office operations. By contrast, the computer has been a tool of large organizations. The computer is a very impressive and expensive pencil and very few design firms have been able to afford its golden touch. The expense of using computers and developing programs has handicapped design firms and prevented them from enlarging their capacity up to now. However, new developments in the computer field are making it possible to produce lower cost systems, making them practical for many more design firms.

Another handicap designers and architects face with the computer is emotional reluctance to use it. Designers, with a highly developed intuitive and aesthetic approach to their discipline, are intimidated by the mathematical and verbal skills required. They shy away from using a sophisticated tool they feel they do not understand. However, it is well within their capacity to learn those skills. You cannot necessarily take a computer genius and teach her or him design, but you can teach a designer with mathematical aptitudes to use the computer.

But why use a computer at all if the expense and natural inclination of a designer seems to point away from its use? For this reason: it is the most powerful management tool for handling the volume of important data required to plan interiors. For the tabulation and manipulation of data there is no substitute. The computer is very fast, error free, and absolutely stupid. People, on the other hand, are relatively slow, error prone, and highly creative. The idea is to create a dialogue between people and machines to take advantage of both.

The computer does what designers consider the "dog work," freeing them to put their energies into creative work. Therefore, it is important for designers to understand how to use this tool. Sooner or later designers will have to deal with the computer and realize that computers do not influence design decisions or affect the creative aspects of planning, but it does force them to organize their thoughts.

DEALING WITH THE COMPUTER

Whether it is a massive project taking many years to complete or half a floor for a renovation, the computer can provide valuable ongoing information about cost and space. It gives an orderly system of thought that imposes a discipline in the way that information is collected. Herbert Newmark uses the computer for detailed planning in projects that involve 300 people or more. These projects can go on for years. Without computer tracking in such projects, changes entered over a period of time tend to get confused and data becomes blurred.

The computer enables a design firm to make all kinds of studies and reports. The data can be projected through all planning stages and updated and revised accurately, right through to the end of the project. For example, every time you add a file to a department, the computer will be able to tell you what the cost will be to the department at any design phase and how many square feet to allow. It can also add the file to the inventory and purchase order with its specifications.

Any complex that can be structured into subsets of information can be programmed for the computer. Such programmatic thinking is a simple, automatic way of dealing with more information that can be kept in the mind at any one time. For example, S.O.M. stores information for cost projections based on variables. In hospital planning, animal room costs are different from operating room or machine areas. Some institutions are heavily weighted and may have fifteen neonatal care units and a very small intensive care unit because they are specialists in this area. S.O.M. has created a very sophisticated system especially in the area of costs based on world-wide conditions.

One of the problems limiting computer use is that many design offices cannot make the tremendous effort in funds and time it requires. Using the computer means structuring information collected into a useful data base and the development of systematic work techniques. It can take years to develop the groundwork on which the computer functions before you can push a button and have it perform. The programs and information stored in the basic data bank will contain all the experience, information and vocabulary the design firm uses as its basic tools. The long-range function is to provide a set of ongoing documents.

Once the data is there it can be processed in many ways. The trick is in programming the computer to get back what you want. There are two basic sets of programs. One deals with numbers and words. The other deals with graphics.

PROGRAMS USING NUMBERS AND WORDS

Programs using numbers and words are the area of greatest practical application. These are the programs which seek to keep up with the mountains of data on people, products, materials, and costs and to automate office chores.

Whether the computer is used in planning, budgeting, or specifications writing, the material fed into it is based on numbers and words. This material is organized in terms of standards, subsets of standards, and variables. It is the way designers have always organized their thinking whether using a computer program or not.

The words and numbers computer program does everything design offices have always done manually up to now. It offers no new concepts for designers to learn except it has made a tremendous improvement in the analytic process. What it does — the tabulation and manipulation of numbers — it does supremely well. The program fulfills its long-range function of providing an ongoing set of documents that result eventually in complete inventory and purchase orders. For example, the computer can be programmed to provide information in the form of reports or data on the following:

   1. Forecasts of company growth based on previous growth periods.

   2. Analysis of space needs by year based on space standards and expansion requirements.

   3. Traffic studies which include communication of people and the flow of paper and information used to decide adjacency of departments.

   4. Analysis of proposed site, taxes, utilization rates, and so on.

   5. Space requirements based on standard situations by department needs and/or by work standards multiplied by personnel count.

6. Space requirements based on nonstandard situations of equipment or special facilities.

7. Budget based on standard and nonstandard equipment.

8. Budget based on construction costs.

9. Lists and summaries printed.

10. Inventories by size, color, style, condition, and location.

11. Inventories by room or area indicating existing equipment or new equipment.

12. Specifications and purchase orders indicating vendor and room location.

13. Tags for moving furniture to new location printed.

14. Inventory of space allocations maintained and assigned for separate housekeeping systems.

Another important contribution that the computer makes is that it eliminates much of the time-consuming tedious typing and checking that must be done to produce the studies, reports, summaries, specifications, and purchase orders. This output is produced accurately and rapidly by the computer. "With a computer," said Herbert Newmark, "you do not have clerical mistakes. Most projects involve multiple use of base statistical data and this requires huge amounts of checking. Who does all the checking? Not low level people. It is done by the architects and designers who are responsible. You don't delegate that to a clerk." Elimination of this tedious work frees designers for the creative work that no one else can do.

PROGRAMS USING GRAPHICS

The types of programs that deal with graphics are the most spectacular and dazzling, but are of limited application to date. Reports in magazines and seminars have come from a few firms relating their experiences. Perry, Dean, and Stewart in Boston, S.L.S. Environetics in New York and Los Angeles, Herman Miller's Decision Resource Service in Zeeland, Michigan, and Nitschke, Godwin, and Bohm in Columbus, Ohio, to name a few are design and architecture firms that have had experience with computer graphics.

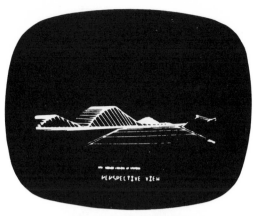

COMPUTER-AIDED DESIGN

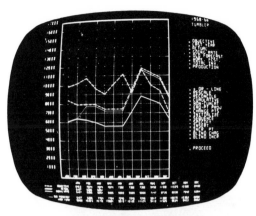

MANAGEMENT PLANNING

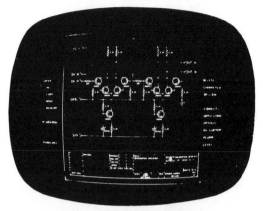

AUTOMATIC DRAFTING

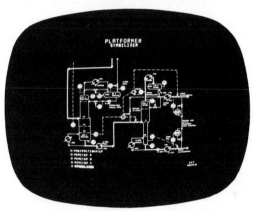

SYSTEMS MONITORING AND CONTROL

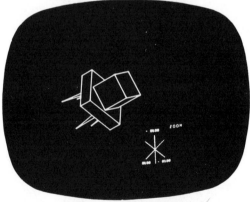

PRODUCT SIMULATION

DATA RETRIEVAL

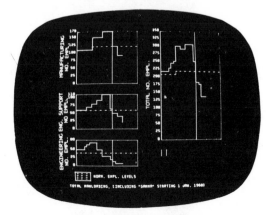

PRODUCTION PLANNING

Fig. 21. **Typical program applications in computer graphics.**
(Courtesy Information Displays, Inc.)

Fig. 22. **Interactive display system.**
(Courtesy Information Displays, Inc.)

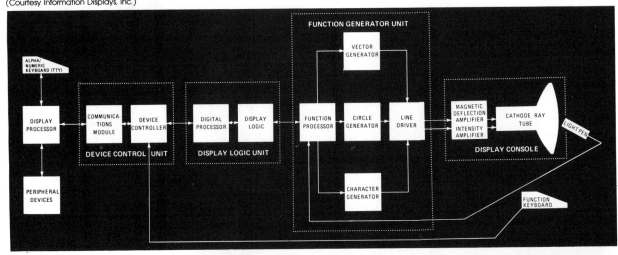

Fig. 23. **Diagram of an interactive computer driven drafting system proposed for a U.S. Army computer design center.**
(Courtesy U.S. Army/Edgewood Arsenal)

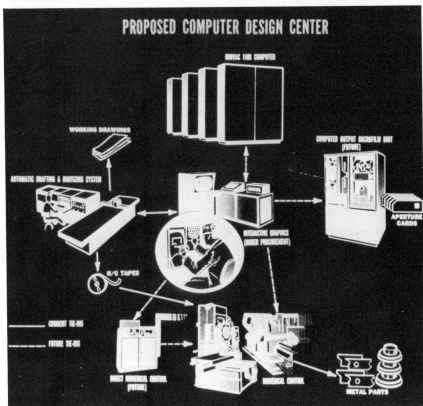

Fig. 24. **Cathode ray tube being used with a light pen for space planning.**
(Courtesy Information Displays, Inc.)

Fig. 25. **A large flatbed plotter manufactured by a division of McDonnell-Douglas Corporation. This unit is capable of producing extremely high quality, high accuracy engineering drawings.**
(Courtesy Information Displays, Inc.)

The word "graphics" has a number of different meanings. In printing, graphics can mean the character font. It can mean diagrams, lines, and pictures used for illustration. It can mean the art of representing a three-dimensional object in a two-dimensional manner. Computer graphics can mean all of these (Fig. 21).

A graphics program makes use of an array of devices that interact with and are operated by computers (Figs. 22 and 23). The images are presented on screens and/or plotters. Devices used are:

    1. Cathode ray tube (CRT) which is a display screen on which the image appears (Fig. 24).

    2. XY plotters which are computer-driven drafting machines (Fig. 25).

Fig. 26. **An interactive computer graphics system, "MAN-MAC" (man plus machine), being used to compute assignable areas of irregular configurations.**
(Courtesy S.L.S. Environetics)

3. Graphic tablets which are used to pick up and store images (Fig. 26).

That is the hardware. It is sophisticated hardware and has been in use for sometime now. Its application in architecture and design has been slow.

Graphics computer applications began in the fifties. The Air Force used the light pen and interactive CRT to affect the computer program. The next major step developed the technology that is still in existence. Ivan Sutherland, at M.I.T., in the early sixties, developed "Sketchpad," a problem-solving device to get more information from a data base using interactive graphics. Architectural programs have been developed that could draw three-dimensional solids, rotate perspectives, and do line drawings and halftone renderings. Today, these are considered expensive frills and do not appear to be useful or practical for space planning, although current technology may eventually reduce costs.

Lawrence Lerner said that he didn't know if computers for graphics is here to stay, on the basis of economic evaluation. Not only does it require very sophisticated hardware, but it also requires countless hours of experimentation and development in software. The science of computer graphics attracts a very small segment of graduating architects.

Fig. 27. **Computer-driven plotter in the New York offices of SLS Environetics. It was developed to produce precision working drawings and floor plans. Lawrence Lerner (on right) has been involved with developing a practical tool for drafting since 1963.**
(Courtesy of S.L.S. Environetics)

It is the rapidity of any computer system that makes it possible to increase the productivity of the user. If you start from scratch, without a data base, the system is not actually faster than manual methods. It may even be slower. But once you have a basis from which to work, there is a tremendous increase in ability. S.L.S. Environetics (Fig. 27) and Perry, Dean and Stewart are among the only ones in the field of architecture and design that can produce computer-drawn working drawings. S.L.S. Environetics has been working at it for sometime now and is not completely satisfied. They use the computer as a means of enhancing the designer's ability to draw.

Studies of mechanical drawing systems claim that they can increase productivity of an individual by five to ten times. Using the computer to drive an XY plotter is, theoretically, simply a way of drafting things more rapidly. The computer graphic system works quickly and accurately to produce drawings to make changes very quickly. The drafting ability of the plotter is a logical way to eliminate the tedious repetitiveness of working drawings and insure their accuracy.

Examples of tasks that a graphic program can do are as follows:

   1. Draw subjects as a variety of scales in full detail with labels and dimensions.

2. Use standard graphic elements as directed.

3. Calculate areas and dimensions, gross or usable.

4. Make drawings that require repetition of many units.

5. Layout sign graphics with automatic spacing and proportion.

6. Lay out stairs that meet codes and convenience.

7. Lay out auditorium seating with good sight lines.

8. Produce bubble diagrams based on data using several criteria.

9. Produce relationship indices, based on adjacencies, visual contacts, frequency of interaction, and so on.

10. Store building plans for recall and quick retrieval of information.

11. Superimpose items in drawings for correlation, such as telephone, lighting, and furniture.

SPACE ALLOCATION PROGRAMS

Programs have been developed to study relationships. These programs work with the interaction of people, measuring frequency distribution, similar to the programs used in sociometric studies. Questionnaires yield information on adjacencies, visual contact, frequency of communications, and so on. This data is entered into the computer to produce bubble diagrams. In turn, the computer can translate this into spatial relationships by attempting to give gross square footage equivalents to create block allocations by departments. Within departments, the program can locate individual work stations. These techniques tantalize designers by offering so much promise. The promise is that designers, abetted by the computer, can accomplish vast amounts of detailed planning accurately and reasonably in very little time. As a practical matter, it does not seem to be replacing the methods that most designers commonly use.

Bubble diagrams are an old and useful tool for analysis and presentation purposes. They are useful both as a theoretical and as a conceptual tool. But for computer space allocation programs, dealing in real world situations, the theoretical must be made to fit the building that has been planned. The appraisal of the constraints of the program and then the feeding of those constraints into the program is a doubly time-consuming job. The accuracy of information is always suspect and open to manipulation. In addition, the computer can give an infinite variety of solutions to go with those constraints. If it is limited to a reasonable number of solutions that can be reviewed practically, they still must be appraised individually to find the best out of the lot. Not only is that time consuming, but it is apt not to be the best solution.

SO YOU WANT TO COMPUTERIZE

After carefully weighing what the computer can do and cannot do, design firms contemplating this step have found some short-cuts to building a program.

There are a few programs in the public domain. Most of these programs have been developed by University research groups. For example, Nitschke, Godwin and Bohm, utilizing a time-sharing arrangement, use a program developed at Ohio State University that the firm has modified over the years. "Computer Architecture Programs," a three-volume set of looseleaf note-books put out by the Boston Center for Environmental Research, lists just about every computer program having to do with architecture. Each program is documented, illustrated, and categorized. The programs are grouped by function such as Building Spaces and Area Analysis, Space Allocation, and so on. Master specifications are available as well. MASTERSPEC was developed by the A.I.A. and is kept current for subscribers. Many university computer centers offer computer time and assistance. Other sources of computer time are with service bureaus, who rent their technicians and skills along with time on the computer.

Some large firms have developed computer programs and are leasing time and expertise to small offices. Small offices can tie into consulting companies around the country. Carl Machover, of Information Displays, Inc., a pioneering firm in the field of interactive graphics, said that systems currently available can cost from one to four times the dollars per hour as the user costs. He described the ideal users of turn-key systems as those firms that have annual revenues of $20 million or more and drafting departments with at least twenty men. But architectural and design firms are small offices. They can afford these tools only if they set up time-sharing cooperatives. Professional organizations could contribute by developing programs that would draw on the combined experiences of the design community and would be made available to the entire profession.

chapter seven
paper
flow

THE PAPER DRAGON

Paper is used to transmit information. Paper is the dragon in the office. It causes quiet chaos. The paper dragon is fed from electronic data processing equipment and office copiers and from handwritten memos and typed products of the word processing centers. The paper then flows into filing equipment and storerooms. The power of the paper dragon dramatically brought Wall Street to a paperwork crisis in the summer of 1968.

While designers have been paying attention to the importance of communication between employees, not enough of our attention has been focused on the single aspect of paper flow. Paper flow stems from the creation and disbursement of data. This data is received, processed, transferred, and stored.

The burst of growth in the textile and railroad industries in the 1880's shaped the modern office. That growth created accounting and record-keeping problems as offices grew in size and complexity. Gradually, machines were introduced to the office to do specialized work. Writing and calculating were being done by machines faster and more efficiently.

The typewriter, introduced about one hundred years ago, affected all office procedures and was the forerunner of all other key driven machines. The evolution of the typewriter illustrates the impact of sophisticated equipment on the office. A brief history of this evolution can be found in Chapter 12. It has created the conditions for unprecedented change. The development of word processing centers in the early 1970's explosively altered the production of paperwork. It has affected the social patterns of the office as well. The dependence on specialized office machines and the increased demand for sophisticated equipment is found wherever paperwork has proliferated such as in law firms, insurance companies, financial institutions, health care centers, government, and corporate offices.

Fig. 28. **The Toledo Edison Word Processing Center — dictation is relayed into the center from either inside or outside the company and stored on tape for transcription.**
(Courtesy IBM Office Products Division)

WORD PROCESSING

Driven by the classic factors of saving time and labor and increasing accuracy, the influence of factory methods on the office began to be felt in the area of clerical work. The changes being brought about will be felt by designers in areas requiring special study. The office is a word processing factory. The word processing concept originated with automating typing procedures.

Some have called it a systems approach to hard-copy communications flow. The mechanics involved are based on the use of magnetic tape electric typewriters which were originally developed by IBM in the early 1960's. Copy is dictated to a specialist in typing who makes a rough transcript on magnetic tape, magnetic card, or paper punch tape. The corrected transcript is used to edit the tape. The final copy is typed out automatically and corrected on a high speed automatic typewriter.

Word processing is also based on the efficiency of machine dictation (Fig. 28). The average speed of machine dictation is sixty words per minute. That is three times the productivity of penmanship since a person can write at the rate of fifteen words per minute. Machine dictation is twice as efficient as face-to-face dictation, assuming an uninterrupted stenographic rate of thirty words per minute. The typist becomes a keyboard specialist, making the original transcription and the corrections. The corrected document is automatically retyped at high speed by remote control while the typist may perform other tasks during the playout of longer documents.

Since this equipment is expensive, the value to an organization must be greater than rapid production of corrected typing. Word processing is that and much more. When typing volume is heavy or where revisions are frequent, magnetic media machines accelerate production. It promotes efficient use of skilled typing personnel by a division of work concept that establishes word processing centers. These work centers are based on the unimpeded flow of work not dependent on a one-to-one relationship. Incidentally, this frees secretaries to advance to administrative management positions. Under word processing, a secretary or keyboard specialist doesn't serve an executive but works for a company, earning raises and promotions through the word processing centers.

What does this mean for the space planner? The word processing center is not the same as the familiar well-established typing pool. Because it requires organizational change as a result of altering the secretarial function, a management commitment to expensive equipment and a method of working, it affects the pattern of communication and work flow that are basic to space planning.

In the word processing center, designers must accommodate the user, the hardware, and the specific problems faced there. The equipment used in word processing is very new, and the space for work stations needed in the center should be flexible to allow for growth. The center should be treated in as open and flexible a way as conditions permit. Fatiguing sound from the machines is probably the biggest problem and it is best handled with the use of carpet on the floor, along with other acoustic controls.

Carpeting is often used in open offices, but in the word processing center its acoustical contribution is increased if it is specified in a heavier face weight than it would ordinarily be needed in relation to wear. This heavier face weight must be balanced with the need to have casters move easily over the surface without using chair pads. The chair pads would only reflect sound and defeat the purpose of the heavier carpet. More detailed information about acoustic controls can be found in Chapter IX.

Wall surfaces, columns, and screens should also be treated for acoustical control. It is important to use furniture that reverberates as little as possible, particularly avoiding work surfaces that are cantilevered or hung from screens or partitions. Freestanding work surfaces for machines and equipment are usually best. They transmit less sound by reverberation and provide a surface that will not warp or wrack with the weight of the equipment. Partitions between work stations tend to reduce distraction but they should be low, if used at all, to allow important human contact during this very mechanical work process.

Word processing consists of the input equipment of dictation and the output equipment of automatic typewriters and text editors. Associated office equipment, such as copiers, storage cabinets, and files, can also be in the areas adjacent to it. The technology of the system should be provided for by the designer and the systems consultant in advance, as it requires provisions for connecting special telephone lines, computer connections, and sophisticated equipment. The dictating equipment may be one of the following:

1. Desktop units — recording physically carried to secretary or word processing center for transcription.

2. Wired system — microphone or phonelike instrument at originator's desk, recorder at secretary's desk or word processing center.

3. Telephone system — uses telephone network, records in word processing center.

4. Message system — same as the telephone system but accepting dictation from outside telephones.

The automatic typing system consists of a keyboard and printer, usually the IBM "Selectric," around which most manufacturers have built their editing logic equipment to be used with the typewriter. They stand alone next to the desk or work surface. Text editing devices sometimes have cathode ray tube (CRT) displays.

ADMINISTRATIVE SUPPORT CENTERS

The two classic work functions of the secretary have been broken down into two areas: (1) typing, and (2) administrative support. Typing duties are taken over by keyboard specialists in the word processing center and administrative needs are often assigned to administrative support centers (Fig. 29).

The concept of administrative support stations makes sense in both conventional office layouts (Fig. 30) and in open office planning (Fig. 31). The station acts as a telephone center, local library, duplicating center, mailroom, file center, stationery and supply depot, and secretarial service center. In an adminis-

Fig. 29. **An administrative center in one of IBM's own facilities provides both correspondence and administrative services for up to six managers in the immediate area. The end wall and the low partitions are covered in carpet.**
(Courtesy IBM Office Products Division)

Fig. 30. **Administrative support area at the office of Coopers and Lybrand, Washington, D.c.**
(Courtesy S.L.S. Environetics)

Fig. 31. **Mercedes-Benz of North America established a central floor service station in their landscaped headquarters. Adjacent to the core, it serves as a reception area and distribution point for mail and supplies which are easily available from transparent racks. It is also the location of the copying machine. This centralized area serves an entire floor.**
(Courtesy Mercedes-Benz of North America)

trative support center, the term "secretary or clerk" is archaic. The new administrative support personnel are more versatile and more highly skilled.

By using modular filing, storage, and library equipment, designers can consolidate and utilize storage space in conjunction with the functioning of the administrative support area. Each area can consolidate a great deal of scattered storage space (Fig. 32).

Modularity in storage units is not a novelty to designers, but consolidation of the storage function into much more than a record room is a new idea. The concept of administrative support areas brings together many more additional functions, other than recordkeeping. Since the area is served by skilled support personnel, the trend is toward open files with color record identification. Access to libraries of information compressed as on microfilm can be housed and supervised along with conventional library materials of books, catalogue binders, and samples.

We are still a paper-oriented society. The last decade has seen an increase in paper work, red tape, government regulations, communications equipment, information, and misinformation. Robert A. Shiff, president of Naremco Services and a consultant in records management, said, "There is no evidence that non-paper oriented equipment, such as microfilm, the computer, or the cathode ray tube (CRT) will have any great impact on reducing the volume of paper work."

Designers and management are increasingly working with consultants such as Robert Shiff. These consultants provide the data and analysis that help determine support facilities and the kinds of filing equipment needed. They can provide the precise measurement of inches of space required for different forms of documentation and recommend the physical location in the plan.

PAPER STORAGE

In storage, as in everything else, the system must be tailormade for the user. The nature of human beings is to want to have things at hand. Almost all people are visually oriented. They want and

need to have something to see and refer to in writing. Designers cannot fight the squirrel instinct but they can provide a system that is responsive to providing information. Centralized filing systems tend to break down the further you get from the location. Every employee will start keeping their own files if they are removed from an administrative support center. Therefore, the support centers should be decentralized and serve the needs of groups of people.

Table 9. **FILE EQUIPMENT ANALYSIS FORM**

File Equipment Analysis is used to gather information about available storage in lineal feet, including shelving, closets, file drawers, computer data storage areas, and vaults. This is supplemented with a questionnaire for personnel that gathers other data. The information is analyzed and used to set up systems for retaining information, for utilizing information more effectively, and equally important, for disposing of useless information. Robert A. Shiff, a leading consultant in records management developed this records survey and has generously made it available.

(Courtesy Naremco Services, Inc.)

FILE EQUIPMENT ANALYSIS — WORKSHEET

COMPANY

DEPARTMENT/SECTION

PRESENT EQUIPMENT

Qty. Cabinets	Total Drawers (Shelves)	Total Capacity (Cu. Ft.)
Std. Letter		
Std. Legal		
Lateral Letter		
Lateral Legal		
Shelf Files		
Plan Files		
Special		

EQUIPMENT CODES

STANDARD FILE CABINETS

A
	Letter Size
A_5	5 drawer
A_4	4 drawer
A_3	3 drawer
A_2	2 drawer

B
	Legal Size
B_5	5 drawer
B_4	4 drawer
B_3	3 drawer
B_2	2 drawer

LATERAL FILE CABINETS

I
	Letter Size
1_5	5 drawer
1_4	4 drawer
1_3	3 drawer
1_2	2 drawer

L
	Legal Size
L_5	5 drawer
L_4	4 drawer
L_3	3 drawer
L_2	2 drawer

MISCELLANEOUS

B.C.	Book Case
C_t	Tab Card
SS	Shelving, Steel
Sw	Shelving, Wooden
S.C.	Supply Cabinet
T	Tub File

PLAN FILES

P
Ph_1	Horizontal 1"
Ph_2	Horizontal 2½"
P_v	Hanging
P_r	Roll Files
P_s	Special

	PRESENT UTILIZATION			REDUCTION (EST.)		
	Volume Records (Cu. Ft.)	Volume Supplies (Cu. Ft.)	Volume Unused (Cu. Ft.)	Transfer Rec. Ctr.	Destroy (Office)	Volume Remaining (Cu. Ft.)
TOTALS	C.F.	C.F.	C.F.	C.F.	C.F.	C.F.

REMARKS

_____

_____

_____

_____

_____

_____

_____

_____

_____

DEPARTMENT MANAGER REVIEW   DATE

RECOMMENDED EQUIPMENT

Qty. Cabinets	Total Drawers (Shelves)	Total Capacity (Cu. Ft.)
Std.		
Std.		
Lateral		
Lateral		
Shelf Files		
Plan Files		
Special		
TOTALS		C.F.

A records survey is essential to establish what space needs will be. Reproduced here are forms developed by the National Records Management Council of New York (Table 9). Preliminary research usually includes an inventory of file equipment and a questionnaire.

Paper handling and the system that is used affects the use of space. The introduction of administrative support centers has affected paper storage by consolidating files. It has also affected how space is allocated to other services. In addition, mail handling and distribution surveys can lead to conclusions that will affect the final design solution. We can trace how the client's needs affect the plan and shape the building by looking backwards again to the example of Time Inc. Although contemporary examples abound and Time, Inc.'s paper distribution system may seem unsophisticated compared to what is available now, it still serves as a model of analysis.

Gerald Luss talked about Time Inc. as follows:

In doing the survey of their personnel and paper handling, we found that they were using some seventy-five people in their mail and messenger department to distribute mail in their old quarters. As far as Time Inc. was concerned this was absolutely an untouchable area. They had refined their information distribution system, their mail system, because it was of utmost importance to them. When something came in over the Washington Bureau news wire, for example, it had to be distributed to twenty different people in the news room in Time Magazine, the news room in Life Magazine, and up to Luce and other top executives. This was paramount to them. It was before telecopies. As a result they had a mailroom operation for each of the magazines and units, including the executives, so there were seven different mailroom operations.

We did a study as part of the evolution of the design and planning concept of the building that recommended to Time Inc. that instead of utilizing space on the upper prime rent floors, that we utilize the third subbasement underground for the receipt of mail and its sorting. We recommended the use of a conveyor system to be designed as part of the building. All of this work was being done prior to the evolution of the final architectural plans for the building.

Time Inc. had agreed that the building should reflect their needs.

Designs for Business proposed putting in a vertical shaft that would accommodate the bulk mail handling conveyor belt, a wire basket type of thing. It could be programmed in the basement mail room to drop off things at the appropriate floor. And that on each of the fifteen floors that they would then occupy, a single mail clerk in a small cubicle, could take care of the mail. We showed that it could be done much quicker from the time the mail would come in to the third basement and get deposited and distributed on the floor, compared to their old system where the mail would be broken down and brought to seven different mail rooms with a crew of people in each. Instead of needing seventy-five people we felt a crew of forty-four could do the work.

We further showed them the savings in salary for this system. It would take 1½ years to recoup the cost of that particular mail system and from then on for the length of the lease, which was at that time twenty-five years, they were home free in terms of that savings. The plan was adopted.

chapter eight
designing
the light
environment

HUMAN FACTORS

The title of this chapter was adapted from a program given at the University of Wisconsin in September 1975. An ambitious undertaking called "Designing the Color, Light and Visual Environment for Human Performance" reported on the research by illuminating engineers, the research in human factors by the National Aeronautics and Space Administration (NASA) and others, and the psychological research by behavioral scientists. It reflected the intense interest in understanding how people interact and are influenced by their environment.

The people in the work space are the subjects of examination by illuminating engineers, human factors engineers, lighting consultants, and designers. These specialists focus on improving the visual environment for human performance. C. Ray Smith said in an editorial in Interiors Magazine that this attention to people and their tasks "illuminates a new humanism."

Humanism is and always was a part of designing for people. Now that environmental psychologists and behaviorists are contributing to design theory, do designers find their contributions significant in terms of the user? Is their information meaningful? Designers can examine their contribution to design theory in two areas: first, the psychological, and second, the physiological responses to color and light. The conclusions that follow may disappoint many.

Wesley Woodson, president of Man Factors, Incorporated, a human factors engineering consulting firm, outlined the human factors approach to structuring the color and light environment. It is based on measuring user needs both physiologically and psychologically. It is concerned with human responses to color and light that are primarily physiological, such as changes in blood pressure, pulse rate, and hormonal activity, changes in the eye such as pupil size, the shape of the lens, and responses of the retinal nerve endings that affect the sensitivity of the eye to light and color.

"There have been numerous studies aimed at determining how color and light affect people physiologically. Except for the case of the actual visual system, however, it is difficult to draw general conclusions. For example, there are conflicting data with regard to the effect of color on body temperature, on aggressiveness, etc.," said Mr. Woodson.

The psychological realm can play an enormously important role in conditioning people to what they perceive and what they will accept as being satisfactory. All of these variables make it difficult to provide a desired psychological response to color and light that is compatible with well-defined mood objectives.

Wesley Woodson concludes, "Above all, we have to see before we can perform visual tasks properly or expect any effect on the observer's mood. Therefore, although mood objectives are important, visual efficiency is a first priority in determining a proper light and color environment."

The organic physiological effects of light will be discussed later in this chapter, but as far as color and the effects of color, the conclusions are inescapable. Designers cannot support a color theory based on psychological reactions or physiological reactions. They must discard as unfounded and useless those color theories that deal with "pleasantness or unpleasantness," which are mood qualities. Color remains a personal symbol, meaningful only to that individual, because of the manifold subjective differences in associations that depend on nature, convention, traditions, age, and social activities.

For a theory based on simpler behavior observations, we can turn to the work of Dr. Richard F. Haines. Dr. Haines has worked as a NASA research scientist at the Ames Research Center, studying how light and vision affect job performance. One of Dr. Haines' primary theses is that the use of color in our environment can play an important role in providing for optimal stimulation, varied yet positive personal satisfaction, and, in general, a socially compatible life style. He thinks that color and light can be used to achieve a desired degree of stimulation and satisfaction.

One aspect of light is color — a tiny fraction of electromagnetic energy called **the visible spectrum**. The normal eye can discriminate more than ten million wavelengths. What we call color is the result of these wavelengths of energy as perceived by our light sensitive retina. To perceive a colored surface, there must be illumination present. We lose the ability to perceive color if there is not enough light.

One fundamental aspect of color and light design is that light

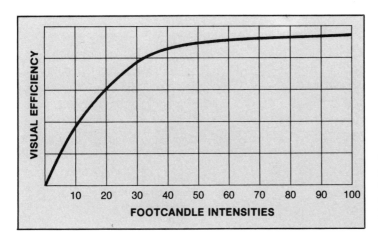

VISUAL EFFICIENCY

FOOTCANDLE INTENSITIES

Table 10. **VISUAL EFFICIENCY RELATED TO ILLUMINATION**

Visual efficiency rises as illumination intensity is raised to a level from 30 to 50 foot candles. After this, improvements in seeing may require multifold increases in light levels.
(Courtesy Man Factors, Inc.)

stimulates people. Dr. Haines says that light increases alertness and that relaxation is usually associated with dimly lit interiors. He feels that the longer one must be in a situation of too much or too little stimulation, the more stressful it can become. This can affect even highly motivated people who will show signs of impaired internal and external performance.

This is something designers have been aware of, having learned it intuitively. What we are looking for in a color theory still eludes us. Designers want to know how a person will react to the fact that we put a particular color in front of them, how does the color affect the work tasks being done, how does the color affect the person if it is perpendicular or oblique to their line of sight. That is how behavioral science can help a designer create a color environment that meets the needs of the user.

QUALITY AND QUANTITY

The quality and quantity of light is important and necessary for visual efficiency (Table 10). Designers are beginning to differentiate between lighting the task and the general lighting needed to promote visual efficiency (Tables 11 and 12).

The problem of how to promote visual efficiency while providing light at the task and general lighting in the flexible

Table 11. **ILLUMINATION LEVELS FOR TASK CONDITIONS**
(Courtesy Man Factors, Inc.)

SPECIFIC RECOMMENDATIONS, ILLUMINATION LEVELS

LOCATION	LEVEL (foot candles)	LOCATION	LEVEL (foot candles)
Home:		*School:*	
Reading	40	On chalkboards	50
Writing	40	Desks	30
Sewing	75-100	Drawing (art)	50
Kitchen	50	Gyms	20
Mirror (shaving)	50	Auditorium	10
Laundry	40		
Games	40	*Theatre:*	
Workbench	50	Lobby	20
General	10 or more	During intermission	5
		During movie	0.1
Office:			
Bookkeeping	50	*Passenger Train:*	
Typing	50	Reading, writing	20-40
Transcribing	40	Dining	15
General correspondence	30	Steps, vestibules	10
Filing	30		
Reception	20	*Doctor's Office:*	
		Examination room	100
		Dental-surgical	200
		Operating table	1800

Table 12. **ILLUMINATION LEVELS FOR GENERAL LIGHTING CONDITIONS**
(Courtesy Man Factors, Inc.)

GENERAL ILLUMINATION LEVELS

TASK CONDITION	LEVEL (foot candles)	TYPE OF ILLUMINATION
Small detail, low contrast, prolonged periods, high speed, extreme accuracy	100	Supplementary type of lighting. Special fixture such as desk lamp.
Small detail, fair contrast, close work, speed not essential	50-100	Supplementary type of lighting.
Normal desk and office-type work	20-50	Local lighting. Ceiling fixture directly overhead.
Recreational tasks that are not prolonged	10-20	General lighting. Random room light, either natural or artificial.
Seeing not confined, contrast good, object fairly large	5-10	General lighting.
Visibility for moving about, handling large objects	2-5	General or supplementary lighting.

A

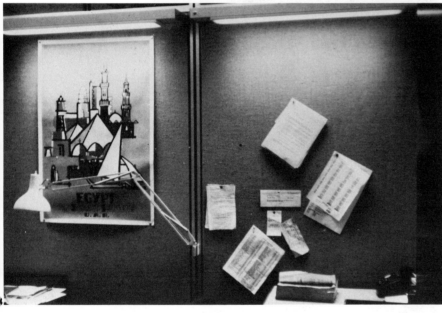

Fig. 33. **Lighting designed by Gerald Luss for Time, Inc., in 1959. It consisted of a moveable modular unit that attached to the wall partition to provide general lighting (A). It was supplemented by an additional moveable lighting unit that could be directed at the task (B).**
(Courtesy Lightolier)

changing office was faced in the classic example of the Time Inc. offices in 1959. The writers and reporters did not like working with glaring or overhead sources of light. They preferred lighting that was at task level — lamp light. To provide overall illumination, Gerald Luss designed an up/down light that fastened to the partition and eliminated the need for light from the ceiling (Fig. 33). It was the forerunner of the work station with built-in task lighting that is being developed today. This was supplemented by portable lighting that could be directed to tasks requiring higher intensity of illumination. The up/down light units, manufactured by Lightolier, could be moved about and put up anywhere. There was a lot of confusion about how to use these lights. It was, at best, a general light but it deserves to be thought of as a forerunner of the more sophisticated up/down lighting that Sylvan Shemitz and others are designing into low partitions and work stations.

Fig. 34. **The Seagram Building at night, illuminated by a twenty-foot perimeter band of light.**
(Courtesy Joseph E. Seagram and Sons, Inc.)

Fig. 35. **The Sears Tower in Chicago. Perimeter lighting is spaced to place a row of lights in pairs behind every window.**
(Courtesy Skidmore, Owings and Merrill)

Fig. 36. **The lighting layout at the Sears Tower in Chicago, on an office floor.**
(Courtesy S.L.S. Environetics)

Today's changes in lighting are a result of many pressures. Among them, the costs of building construction that forced lighting designers to use fewer fixtures and less watts per square foot, the growing conservation movement that was eclipsed by the larger political and economic reality of the Arab oil manipulations, and the need to provide a better visual environment in open offices.

At one time, putting light in every module was exciting. Lighting the perimeter of the Seagram's Building enhanced its elegance. The luminous band of light was part of the design of the precisely honed curtain wall (Fig. 34). The same design objective was used in the Sears Tower but with completely different constraints.

Claude Engle, the lighting consultant, said, "We were simply told that in the budget there was room for one fixture per fifty square feet. We wanted it to relate to the window module, so we began to play with the geometry (Fig. 35). We knew that the partitioned offices would be at the perimeter. That meant that whatever we did with the lighting, it would have to be basically modular around the perimeter. We put a row of lights in pairs behind every window that would be spaced about seven feet apart, so that they cover an office adequately (Fig. 36). That meant one fixture every forty square feet. That left us on the interior of the building with one fixture for every fifty-six square feet. We worked out a plan in which every fifteen foot by fifteen foot open module would have four fixtures, one fixture for every fifty-six square feet. That meant that a combination of the perimeter and interior zones met the fifty square feet criteria. So Sears has a perimeter band with a field in the middle, which worked out beautifully." A further development of this approach was the grouping of fixtures to relate to work areas, and this idea was applied in other installations.

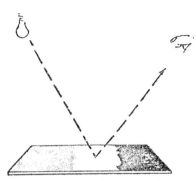

Fig. 37. **When a surface is very hard and glossy, light rays concentrate, making the intensity of the light and apparent brightness of one part of a surface much higher than that of another. This results in a variation in the apparent color of one part of the surface as compared to another. If source intensity is high enough, it is possible to obliterate the color impression altogether, so that the source itself is reflected as "glare."**
(Courtesy Man Factors, Inc.)

Fig. 38. **Lighting built into the work station.**
(Courtesy Knoll International)

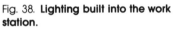

Fig. 39. **Lighting built into file units where the task demands higher light levels.**
(Courtesy Knoll International)

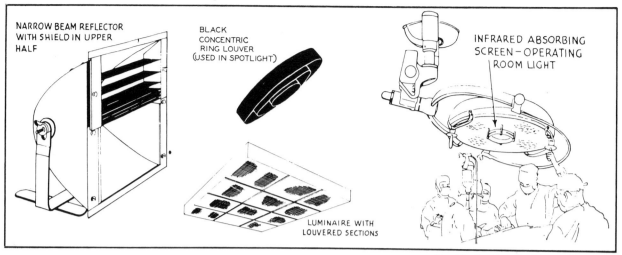

NARROW BEAM REFLECTOR WITH SHIELD IN UPPER HALF

BLACK CONCENTRIC RING LOUVER (USED IN SPOTLIGHT)

INFRARED ABSORBING SCREEN—OPERATING ROOM LIGHT

LUMINAIRE WITH LOUVERED SECTIONS

Fig. 40. **Shades, shields and louvers are used in lighting equipment to absorb and redirect light into useful directions.**
(Courtesy General Electric Lighting Institute)

REFLECTIONS, BRIGHTNESS, AND GLARE

When electricity was plentiful, the easiest way to assure overall lighting in open plan was to install lighting fixtures over an entire ceiling to produce an even spread of light and maintain 100-foot candles at desk level. We began to be troubled by distracting overhead glare and veiling reflections that limited the effectiveness of the lighting solution that was, at its best, dull and repetitious.

The problem of controlling glare from a light source is important whether the light is coming from a window, from overhead fixtures, or from the work station. To eliminate the distracting bright, overhead glare, the illuminating engineering society recommends using a system of batwing or parabolic baffles. They act to darken the source of light at the ceiling when seen from below and the baffles direct and distribute the light by removing it from the "glare zone." The "glare zone" is considered to be the light in front of the person coming directly down on the work surface and reflected or diffused into that person's eyes (Fig. 37).

Several manufacturers, such as Knoll, Herman Miller, Westinghouse, and Steelcase, have been incorporating strip lighting into their work stations (Fig. 38) and into files and bookshelves (Fig. 39). Light located in the work station can act as task lighting. This light can subject eyes to the same kind of reflection as overhead light. Unfortunately, the ideal position for light in a work station is just above the desk and parallel to it. That puts the light in the worst possible location from the point of view of reflections. Unless light is shielded or baffled to minimize down light and direct the light sideways, serious veiling reflections are created (Fig. 40).

Veiling reflections are the reflections from the light source that obscure vision. It was formerly thought that using matte paper would eliminate this reflection. Interesting microscopic studies

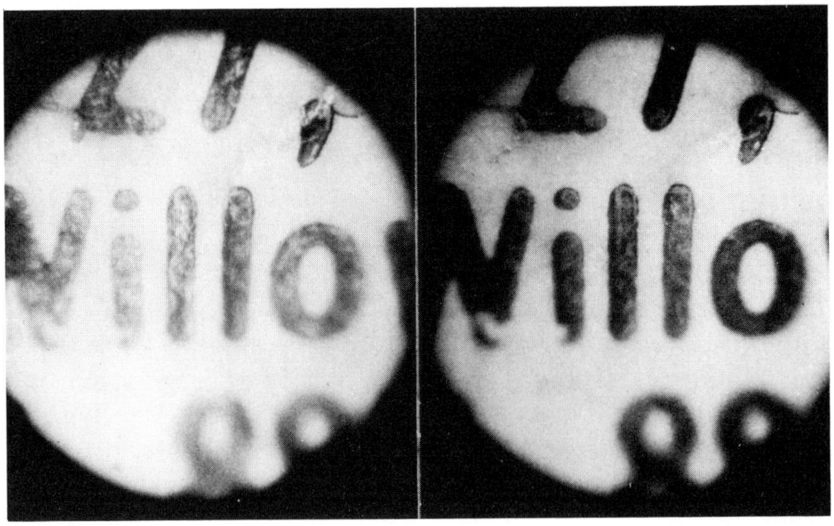

Fig. 41. **Veiling reflections from a lighting source reduce the contrast and obscure the letters in the photograph on the left. On the right, the same sample with the veiling reflections shielded out.**
(Courtesy Illuminating Engineering Research Institute)

show that facets of glossiness exist even in the matte papers. The reflection was under the surface but still there, cutting down the contrast and limiting vision (Fig. 41).

Glare from overhead fixtures not only results in veiling reflections at the work surface but it also gives a sense of discomfort when a person looks up. You don't look down all the time, you look up to talk to someone, to check something, or just as a change in head position. Every time you look up and see the brightness of 500 foot lamberts of the fluorescent lens surface on the ceiling, the iris contracts to adapt to it and the iris has to open up again when you look down to the desk with its surface brightness of about 80 foot lamberts. The iris adjustment is not instantaneous. It takes time and slows up visual performance and causes a strain of the eyes' sphincter muscle.

Studies here and abroad have developed a formula to evaluate the discomfort of glare and to eliminate it. The Visual Comfort Probability (VCP) System has been adapted as a standard of performance by the Illuminating Engineering Society. Designers should request the VCP information about any fixture from the manufacturer. It is a very useful tool to compare and evaluate competitive equipment. For example, Lightolier's parabolic cell fixture rated 90 VCP. That means that 90 percent of the people viewing it would find it visually comfortable. It can be compared to another manufacturer's fixture that is being

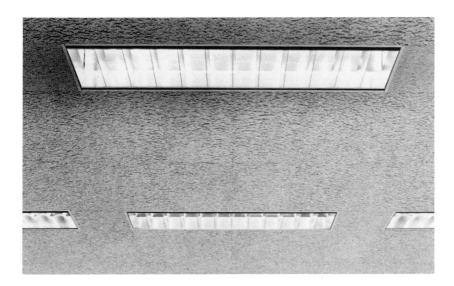

Fig. 42. **A ceiling fixture with a high Visual Comfort Probability (VCP), designed to eliminate the discomfort of glare.**
(Courtesy Lightolier)

advocated for open office use that rates about 40 VCP. The higher the figure, the less the glare (Fig. 42).

THE AMOUNT OF LIGHT ON A TASK

The way an object reflects light is the most important character-istic as far as sight is concerned. The eye sees things only be-cause of reflected light or variations of color, brightness, and shadow.

Research on different elements in the luminous environment is conducted by the Illuminating Engineering Research Institute (IERI) at universities using college students with good vision as their norm. They found that if the surroundings are too low or too high in luminance in relation to that of the luminous task, there is a loss of sensitivity or ability to see. In other words, if there is too much contrast either way from the brightness of the background of the detail, vision suffers. The optimum condition is to illuminate the background and surrounding area equal to the back-ground of detail (Table 13).

Looking up from a brightly lighted task to a dark surrounding or an overly bright surrounding causes eye discomfort and loss of visibility. We know then that the ideal situation is where the sur-

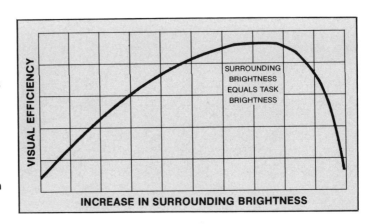

Table 13. **VISUAL EFFICIENCY RELATED TO SURROUNDING BRIGHTNESS**

With the brightness of the task held constant, visual efficiency will increase as the surrounding brightness is raised to a level equal to or slightly lower than the task brightness. Higher surrounding brightness may lead to a collapse in acuity.

(Courtesy Man Factors, Inc.)

(Graph labels: VISUAL EFFICIENCY on vertical axis, INCREASE IN SURROUNDING BRIGHTNESS on horizontal axis, SURROUNDING BRIGHTNESS EQUALS TASK BRIGHTNESS)

roundings are about equal to the background of the detail of the work or there will be a loss of sensitivity as the iris adapts to different areas of luminants. Recommendations have been made by the IERI that the area surrounding the task should not have less than one-third of the luminance of the task, regardless of the amount of light.

This recommendation of the IERI emphasizes the importance of controlling the brightness of the ceiling, whether using indirect light or ceiling fixtures. Ceiling brightness is part of the surrounding environment and should be kept low in relation to the task. If the desk has 50 to 100 foot candles, the surrounding area should be about 30 foot candles.

LEVELS OF LIGHT

The research, based on the reactions of healthy college students with good vision, brings up another important aspect of vision. We all know that our vision changes with time. It does not improve, unfortunately, and our eyes do not maintain the level we had in college. The IERI has determined that in order to maintain visibility equal to the average twenty-year old, we need to dramatically increase the level of light as we get older (Table 14). A thirty-year old needs more light than a twenty-year old to see the task effectively. A fifty-year needs considerably more light than a forty-year old. These personal differences in vision have not been taken into account in designing the light en-

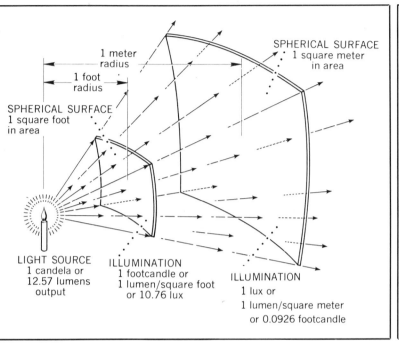

SPHERICAL SURFACE
1 square meter
in area

1 meter
radius

1 foot
radius

SPHERICAL SURFACE
1 square foot
in area

LIGHT SOURCE
1 candela or
12.57 lumens
output

ILLUMINATION
1 footcandle or
1 lumen/square foot
or 10.76 lux

ILLUMINATION
1 lux or
1 lumen/square meter
or 0.0926 footcandle

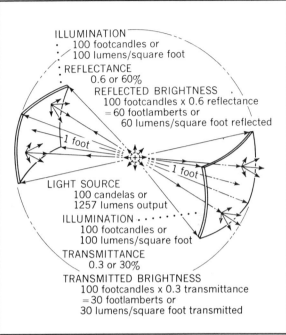

ILLUMINATION
100 footcandles or
100 lumens/square foot

REFLECTANCE
0.6 or 60%

REFLECTED BRIGHTNESS
100 footcandles x 0.6 reflectance
= 60 footlamberts or
60 lumens/square foot reflected

1 foot

1 foot

LIGHT SOURCE
100 candelas or
1257 lumens output

ILLUMINATION
100 footcandles or
100 lumens/square foot

TRANSMITTANCE
0.3 or 30%

TRANSMITTED BRIGHTNESS
100 footcandles x 0.3 transmittance
= 30 footlamberts or
30 lumens/square foot transmitted

Fig. 44. **What we see is the result of light being reflected by a surface. Light is invisible as it travels through space, until it is reflected as surface brightness. There are 2 common units of brightness: candelas per square inch (A), and foot candles (B).**
(Courtesy General Electric Lighting Institute)

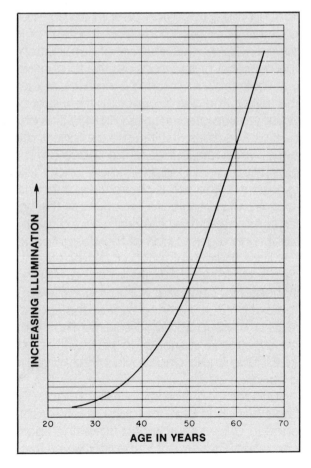

INCREASING ILLUMINATION

AGE IN YEARS

Table 14. **VISUAL CAPABILITY AND AGE**

Eye specialists tell us that visual capability changes with age. IERI research has shown that peak visual performance occurs in the teens and early twenties and goes into steady and increasing decline as one approaches the thirties to the sixties. The graph exemplifies the proportional increase in the light required by a normal-sighted person to maintain a level of vision as age advances. Research is continuing in this interesting relationship to discover the role of other contributing factors.
(Courtesy The Illuminating Engineering Research Institute)

Fluorescent Lamps

Lamp Names	Cool* White	Deluxe* Cool White	Warm** White	Deluxe** Warm White	Daylight	White
Efficacy (Lumens/watt)	High	Medium	High	Medium	Medium-High	High
Lamp appearance effect on neutral surfaces	White	White	Yellowish white	Yellowish white	Bluish white	Pale yellow white
Effect on "atmosphere"	Neutral to moderately cool	Neutral to moderately cool	Warm	Warm	Very Cool	Moderately warm
Colors strengthened	Orange Yellow, Blue	All nearly equal	Orange, Yellow	Red, Orange, Yellow, Green	Green, Blue	Orange, Yellow
Colors greyed	Red	None appreciably	Red, Green, Blue	Blue	Red, Orange	Red, Green Blue
Effect on complexions	Pale Pink	Most natural	Sallow	Ruddy	Greyed	Pale
Remarks	Blends with natural daylight—Good color acceptance	Best overall color rendition; simulates natural daylight	Blends with incandescent light—poor color acceptance	Good color rendition; simulates incandescent light	Usually replaceable with CW	Usually replaceable with CW or WW

* Greater preference at higher levels.   ** Greater preference at lower levels.

vironment. Ideally, there should be individual control over task lighting levels. What a responsive, sophisticated tool we would have then!

THE VISUAL PICTURE

Lighting the task and the work surface is only one small part of lighting the office. Most people do not spend all day looking at a piece of paper. Once the problem of lighting that paper is solved, with a basic amount of illumination and control of glare, the designer has to consider the total area. What you see when you look around a room is a series of pictures. After planning the layout, the designer begins the visual construction of space. What we see are surfaces (Fig. 43). The character of the space begins to express itself in the designer's mind as a series of pictures. When renderings of the space are made, this character is communicated. Designers know what they want light to do and express it in the series of drawings that may never show a light source but do indicate exactly how the light will act on the surfaces of the space. They will show a bright wall or a dark area. Light is an organic part of the design conception even though the light source selection and placement may not have been decided (Table 15). Lighting has an important theatrical component. Not only does it illuminate the space but it dramatizes the action in it. Lighting makes the space interesting and projects a message. It is no surprise that some lighting designers have gained experience in the theatre and in TV. Designers such as Claude Engle and David Mintz have had just such a background.

Surfaces can absorb or reflect light (Fig. 44). Light-colored floors are an important factor in reflectants (Fig. 45). The difference in a light source of a travertine floor versus a dark carpet can equal 35 percent in the light level. The floor can reflect light

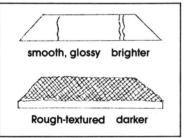

Fig. 43. **Rough-textured surfaces make any color appear darker and less bright because more of the light falling on the surface is absorbed. Conversely a smooth, glossy surface reflects more light, making the color appear brighter.**
(Courtesy Man Factors, Inc.)

	Incandescent	High Intensity Discharge Lamps				
te/Natural	Filament**	Clear Mercury	White Mercury	Deluxe White* Mercury	Multi-Vapor*	Lucalox**
dium	Low	Medium	Medium	Medium	High	High
plish te	Yellowish white	Greenish blue-white	Greenish white	Purplish white	Greenish white	Yellowish
rm kish	Warm	Very cool, Greenish	Moderately cool, Greenish	Warm, Purplish	Moderately cool, Greenish	Warm Yellowish
, Orange	Red Orange Yellow	Yellow Green Blue	Yellow Green Blue	Red Yellow Blue	Yellow Green Blue	Yellow Orange Green
en, Blue,	Blue	Red, Orange	Red, Orange	Green	Red	Red, Blue
ddy Pink	Ruddiest	Greenish	Very pale	Ruddy	Greyed	Yellowish
ted Source ually laceable h CWX or VX	Good color rendering	Very poor color rendering	Moderate color rendering	Color acceptance similar to CW fluorescent	Color acceptance similar to CW fluorescent	Color acceptance approaches that of WW fluorescent

Fig. 45. **Reflected light from walls and floor increase the efficiency of the incandescent fixtures. Shown is a corridor at the National Life and Accident Insurance Company, Nashville, Tennessee.**
(Courtesy Skidmore, Owings and Merrill)

Fig. 46. **The reflective quality of the materials used in the Banco di Roma in Chicago by Skidmore, Owings and Merrill was capitalized by the lighting. Polished Italian black granite floors and stainless steel walls mirror and reflect bright planes and surfaces.**
(Courtesy Claude Engle, Lighting Consultant)

and save energy. There is nothing that can be done to a light fixture that can make 35 percent more light come out; but by using a light colored floor, you can add more light.

Light floors also help control ceiling brightness. The floor will light the ceiling. In the new Avery Fisher Hall, Philip Johnson wants an antique white ceiling to reflect warm light and he will achieve it by using gold carpeting and seats.

In the Banco di Roma, the architect had a visual picture of bright and shining materials. Stainless steel is a mirror and bright planes must be reflected in it to brighten it. A luminous ceiling was installed to give the other surfaces something to reflect (Fig. 46). In the Federal Reserve Building in Washington, the corridors were gloomy, cold and very long. The first thing that was done was to install a light-colored carpet that warmed it up

Fig. 47. **Grouped lighting fixtures over work areas leave the high ceiling dramatically exposed in the New York office of the Gilman Paper Company.**
(Courtesy S.L.S. Environetics)

right away. The proportions seemed to change at the same time. The second step was to light the walls, which made the corridors seem two feet wider. The walls were lit with an inobtrusive low brightness, parabolic type of incandescent down light that had built into its reflector two special reflectors that wash opposite walls, giving light to two parallel walls. The space was transformed into something warm and wide.

Grouping fixtures over work areas achieves lights and darks that have the feeling of customization of lighting (Fig. 47). It can produce lighting that carefully illuminates what you wish but produces lighting that is interesting as you walk around. Low brightness fixtures used in this way seem like down lights. There are no terribly bright objects on the ceiling in deadly rows, going on forever, and there are nice highs and lows in lighting levels.

chapter nine
acoustics

SPEECH AND PRIVACY NEEDS

One of the most controversial aspects of open office planning is the sound and noise pattern. Sound at the wrong time and place is noise. In the office, noise is what interferes with concentration or exposes someone to a sense of an invasion of privacy.

Open office planning should facilitate the way people work together. People who work in a group regardless of rank, and departmental status, should have open and easy access to each other (Fig. 48). This ease of communication is never considered objectionable. Rarely is speech privacy required. Normal speech becomes part of the overall background sound and does not interfere. In the open office, the individuals adjust their voices according to the degree of communication or privacy they feel is necessary. There is no false sense of security.

Executives, who are used to private, walled offices, sometimes feel as though they are losing their privacy and are reluctant to change to the open office. The private office gives a false sense of security, a comfortable imagined privacy to its occupant. In an office with a door to a corridor, the occupant would probably leave the door open 90 percent of the time, and for good reason (Fig. 49). He or she would do it to allow a psychological escape from the confines of the work. He or she can touch with activities in the corridor or outer office and can "look busy" if someone is coming.

The privacy one feels does not apply to acoustics. The noise level in a corridor is usually quite low and the conversation of a person in an office is easily heard. The office door might open to a typing or machine area. Not only does the occupant of a private office have to listen to sounds of the outer office intruding on the environment, but since the outside din is not quite continuous, there will be lapses when sounds from the private office are audible to everyone outside it. Wall construction may be inadequate acoustically. An induction unit or duct work can furnish a path of communication. It is a universal observation, what you hear never sounds half as important or interesting as what you overhear.

It is rare that speech privacy is required in offices of any type, whether partitioned or open. The obvious exceptions are con-

Opposite

Fig. 48. **One of the most successful aspects of this open office at the Port Authority of New York and New Jersey, World Trade Center, is the general low noise level. The open spaces are so large that walls are hardly a factor. Sound is controlled as a result of the carpeted floor, acoustical ceiling, and the high efficiency of sound absorption built into the screens and cabinet backs. All the screens and storage cabinets are independent and non-linking with openings at the center to allow the loose stringing of power and telephone wires.**
(Courtesy Ford and Earl Design Associates)

Fig. 49. **Offices at American Can Company in Greenwich, Connecticut, illustrate the common practice of occupants leaving doors open.**
(Courtesy Skidmore, Owings and Merrill)

103

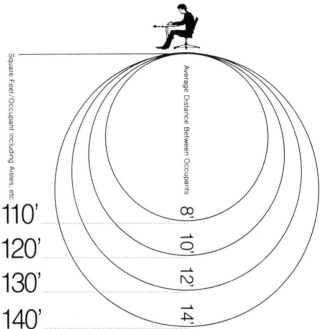

Fig. 50. Sound travels spherically in all directions. Since space is not limited, a range of 110 to 140 square feet per occupant is a reasonable compromise between space usage and noise reduction.
(Courtesy Inter Royal Corporation)

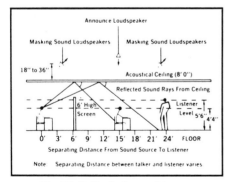

Fig. 51. Reflected sound is distributed over a wide area. The ceiling receives the greatest amount of sound and is the most important surface for control of reflected sound energy.
(Courtesy Robert A. Hansen Associates)

ference rooms and offices used for discussing very confidential information, hiring or firing. When voices are raised, the sound should be controlled. If the boss is bawling someone out, the office should not stop to listen. The main concern is to insure that the conversations and sounds will not interfere with another person's concentration.

In the open office, sounds travel spherically, in all directions, if the sound does not encounter reflecting surfaces like walls, ceilings and floors (Fig. 50). Sound intensity decreases as it leaves the source. Therefore, the further you are from the source, the less you hear. Distance is one way to insure confidentiality. Conversation should be confidential if an unintended listener is sixteen feet away. Maximum acoustical energy occurs directly in front of the speaker. Direct face-to-face or line of sight contact facilitates communication. If greater privacy is desired, the speaker should not face the unintended listener but be to his or her side or back. This concept explains why early German office landscape layouts had a random pattern of desk placement. However, acoustical problems arise for two reasons. One is that the unintended listener is frequently closer than sixteen feet, and

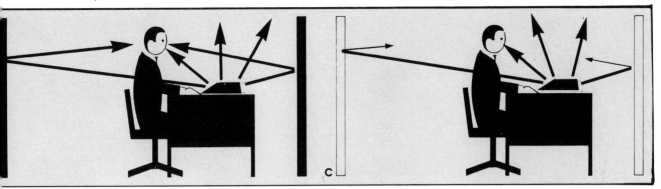

Fig. 52. **Sound travels in all directions from its source. If you are in a completely open environment, the only sound you'll hear comes directly from the source (A). In offices, walls or other hard surfaces reflect sounds. You now hear the original sound and in addition, you hear sound which is reflected to you from the hard surfaces. The noise level has increased drastically as a result of reflected sound (B). If the surfaces surrounding you are absorptive, the sound you hear from the source still exists, but the sounds reflected from the environment are greatly decreased (C).**
(Courtesy Techniques in Wood)

the second reason is that reflective surfaces propagate sound (Fig. 51).

REVERBERATION

Reflective surfaces, whether they are the walls, ceiling, floor, or acoustic panels, create reverberant energy. Its distribution and buildup can be controlled by absorptive materials. Sound absorbing materials not only absorb the sound of the speaker, they also absorb all background masking sounds (Fig. 52).

Sounds bounce off all surfaces within an enclosure in the same manner as a shout will bounce off a mountain and come back as an echo. An echo is a delayed return, delayed because of the distances involved and the time it takes the sound to travel. This is "reverberation time." The sound continues to bounce, losing energy with each reflection. In an office, the distances are less than outdoors. Sounds are reflected from closer surfaces and the reflected sounds do not appear as an echo, but as a reinforcement. The reinforcement creates a gain of sound pressure at a distance from the person speaking, or the machine source. This sometimes can focus the sound at a distance greater than sixteen feet away from the speaker, making her or him audible and intelligible, regardless of the space between the speaker and the listener. The buildup of sound comes from the reflecting surfaces in the space, the ceiling, the floor, the windows, and the walls. The greatest amount of reflected speech is attributed to the ceiling.

The ceiling is an effective area for sound reflection or absorption. It contributes more to the control of sound than vertical surfaces in work stations and acoustic panels. Acoustic treatments on other surfaces supplements the sound absorption properties of the ceiling.

CEILINGS

"To me the two top considerations for acoustical design in the

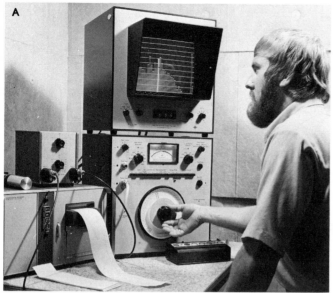

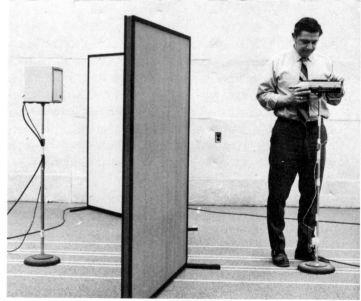

Fig. 53. **In acoustical research much of the definitive testing is done by independent laboratories. The primary reason for this is to provide unbiased reporting of test data. Some manufacturers maintain their own facilities to study architectural acoustics. Instrumentation for testing includes a real time analyzer (A); test set up for objective evaluation of speech privacy in open plan (B); test set up for subjective evaluation of speech privacy in open plan (C); preparing an objective test with an acoustical screen (D).**
(Courtesy Armstrong Cork Company)

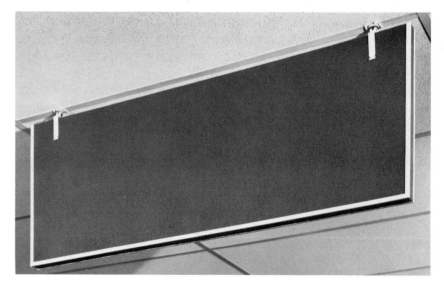

Fig. 54. **Baffles are designed to improve the sound absorbing characteristics of the ceiling.**
(Courtesy Armstrong Cork Company)

open plan are the sound absorptive qualities of the total ceiling and the introduction of masking sound," says Robert Hansen of Robert A. Hansen Associates. "Then comes the separating distance between areas, acoustical shields, walls and floor."

The primary purpose of an acoustical ceiling is to reduce reflected sound energy. There have been many ceiling systems that are successful in open office environments. A ceiling can consist of accoustical tile material, lighting fixtures, and air terminal devices.

Occasionally, the lighting designer and the acoustician must resolve differences that arise over lighting fixtures. Fixtures with lenses can act to reflect sound rather than absorb it. The orientation of the width or length of a lens to the direction of sound energy can vary the quantity of sound energy. Lenseless fixtures provide coffered space to scatter sound. Ideally, lighting fixtures should not occupy more than fifteen percent of the total ceiling area. Acousticians prefer two-by-two fixtures in place of two-by-four fixtures.

The sound absorption of ceiling materials and all other materials is measured by the manufacturer who publishes their performance data (Fig. 53). The ability of a material to absorb sound energy is measured as its Noise Reduction Coefficient, or NRC. An NRC of .99 would indicate almost total absorption. The ideal specifications for an acoustical ceiling system is for an NRC equal to .85 or more. However, in considering the NRC of the ceiling material, it should be thought of as part of the total ceiling system, including the luminaries, the air distribution system, and so on.

It should also be noted that many significant speech frequencies and office machine noises extend beyond the ranges generally considered within the NRC test range. There are people with voices that have both higher and lower frequencies than normally considered within the NRC.

Ceiling baffles can improve the reduction of sound energy within the open office (Fig. 54). Such absorptive panels can be hung beneath the acoustical ceiling system, or used as they were at the Mercedes-Benz headquarters, where twelve-inch deep baffles were suspended eight inches below the slab. (Fig. 55). Ceiling baffles in certain situations can be installed in specific sections of the ceiling to control the sound generated there. Ceiling baffles can make up for deficiencies in acoustical tiles.

Fig. 55. **At the Mercedes-Benz headquarters, the acoustical requirement that a conversation not be overheard beyond 18 feet was met in many ways. The hung ceiling of acoustical baffles in triangular formation provided important control. The ceiling also provides overall luminosity from bare fluorescent luminars without lenses.** (Courtesy Mercedes-Benz of North America)

Pile Height	NRC (mean)
1/8" (.125)	.15
3/16" (.187)	.20
1/4" (.250)	.25
7/16" (.437)	.40

Table 16. **The NRC's of typical commercial carpets in common use laid directly on concrete. Carpet pile weight remains constant while pile height is increased.**
(Courtesy Carpet and Rug Institute)

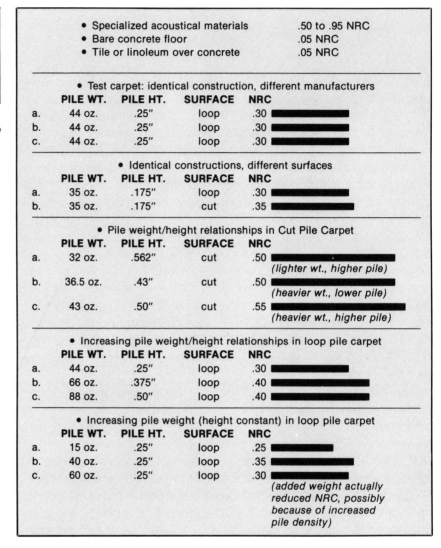

- Specialized acoustical materials .... .50 to .95 NRC
- Bare concrete floor .... .05 NRC
- Tile or linoleum over concrete .... .05 NRC

- Test carpet: identical construction, different manufacturers

	PILE WT.	PILE HT.	SURFACE	NRC
a.	44 oz.	.25"	loop	.30
b.	44 oz.	.25"	loop	.30
c.	44 oz.	.25"	loop	.30

- Identical constructions, different surfaces

	PILE WT.	PILE HT.	SURFACE	NRC
a.	35 oz.	.175"	loop	.30
b.	35 oz.	.175"	cut	.35

- Pile weight/height relationships in Cut Pile Carpet

	PILE WT.	PILE HT.	SURFACE	NRC	
a.	32 oz.	.562"	cut	.50	*(lighter wt., higher pile)*
b.	36.5 oz.	.43"	cut	.50	*(heavier wt., lower pile)*
c.	43 oz.	.50"	cut	.55	*(heavier wt., higher pile)*

- Increasing pile weight/height relationships in loop pile carpet

	PILE WT.	PILE HT.	SURFACE	NRC
a.	44 oz.	.25"	loop	.30
b.	66 oz.	.375"	loop	.40
c.	88 oz.	.50"	loop	.40

- Increasing pile weight (height constant) in loop pile carpet

	PILE WT.	PILE HT.	SURFACE	NRC
a.	15 oz.	.25"	loop	.25
b.	40 oz.	.25"	loop	.35
c.	60 oz.	.25"	loop	.30

(added weight actually reduced NRC, possibly because of increased pile density)

Table 17. **The NRC's of various carpets laid directly on concrete.**
(Courtesy Carpet and Rug Institute)

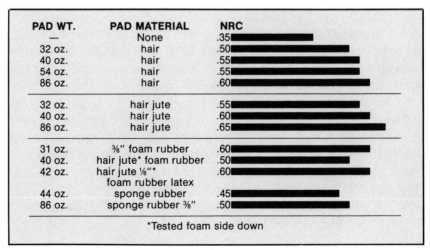

PAD WT.	PAD MATERIAL	NRC
—	None	.35
32 oz.	hair	.50
40 oz.	hair	.55
54 oz.	hair	.55
86 oz.	hair	.60
32 oz.	hair jute	.55
40 oz.	hair jute	.60
86 oz.	hair jute	.65
31 oz.	⅜" foam rubber	.60
40 oz.	hair jute* foam rubber	.50
42 oz.	hair jute ⅛"* foam rubber latex	.60
44 oz.	sponge rubber	.45
86 oz.	sponge rubber ⅜"	.50

*Tested foam side down

Table 18. **The NRC's of various carpets placed over 40-oz. hair cushion.**
(Courtesy Carpet and Rug Institute)

FLOORS

The use of carpet for its acoustical contribution to the open office has been recognized widely. Carpeting is the best material for obtaining sound absorption on the floor, becase it absorbs ten times more sound than any other type of floor covering. Carpeting has a three-fold benefit. First is the reduction of impact noises. Second is efficient sound absorption. Third is the reduction in surface noise.

Efficient sound absorption is measured as the Noise Reduction Coefficient (NRC). The NRC of tile or linoleum over concrete is .05. The NRC of carpets glued directly to a concrete slab ranges between .15 for carpets with a 1/8-inch pile to .40 for carpets with a 7/16-inch pile (Table 16). A cut pile will have a slightly higher NRC than a looped pile of the same construction (Table 17). Different pile yarns do not affect sound absorption. Carpet cushions can add significantly to the NRC, up to .70 if the carpet backing is permeable enough to permit sound energy to penetrate to the cushion (Table 18).

Carpeting contributes significantly to the sound environment of the open office. While it covers an area equal to the acoustic ceiling system, its influence is second to the ceiling.

VERTICAL SURFACES

Vertical surfaces, such as walls, windows, drapes, movable acoustical panels or screens, and work stations, are important because of their potential sound reflecting characteristics. The acoustical material applied to these surfaces should have an NRC equal to .75 or more (Fig. 56). Sound absorptive panels applied to wall surfaces within five feet of business machines can efficiently reduce the noise levels of these machines.

Movable screens used in the open office are possibly the most overly specified item in the environment. They are also the most criticized. Their purpose is to provide a degree of visual and sound separation and to provide additional sound absorption. Ideally, the screens should be within three to five feet of the

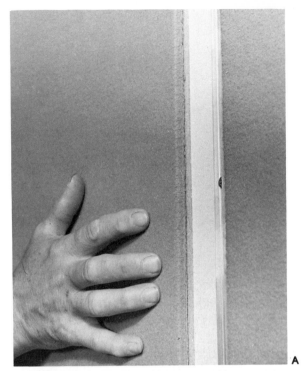

Fig. 56. **Acoustic wall panels are easy to install against dry wall construction (A). Here a worker installs the panel using a special metal spline to hold it in place (B).**
(Courtesy Armstrong Cork Company)

sound source and the listener should be in the acoustical shadow. When that occurs, transmitted sound is reduced.

As an acoustical control, screens seem to have a limited value, since the speaker can be constantly moving and sound is not focused at the screen. The sounds a speaker makes can go over, under, and past the sides of these panels. It has been observed that panels are used by people in the office, not to control sound, but to define territory. Screens encourage the feeling of enclosure. Some people like to cocoon themselves, others like to enlarge their territory by spreading the screens out, encroaching on other's spaces and narrowing aisles. When screens are used to surround each individual they defeat the purpose of open and easy communication.

MASKING SOUND SYSTEMS

Shortcomings in acoustical conditions can be compensated for, within limits, by the use of an electrocoustic masking sound system. This masking sound system interferes with the ability to discern some sounds. The system provides a background sound spectrum designed to achieve speech privacy by basing it on the speech spectrum and the existing noise level of mechanical equipment (Fig. 57).

The levels can vary in any installation. The masking sound is related to the spectrum of sound that is to be covered. The properly designed system should not be noisy or annoying. The resulting sound is like the sound of mechanical equipment, or air conditioning, yet it masks the speech frequency range. Masking sound levels are effective at 45 dBA but cannot be raised to more than 50 dBA without creating intolerable conditions for most people.

In the control of sound, the final result is the sum of all the individual factors. An objective evaluation of the acoustical properties of an area can only be determined by conducting tests within the completed space. The data would indicate the privacy of speech that has been achieved and the need for making adjustments.

In this highly technical field, the General Services Administration's Public Building Service has issued a set of performance standards and performance tests to achieve speech privacy in federal installations. They have issued a two-volume guide "Acoustical Performance Specifications for an Integrated Ceiling and Background System," which details all aspects of this problem. It establishes acceptable performance standards that can be followed by designers.

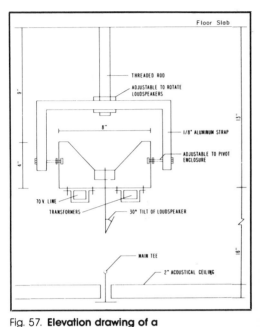

Fig. 57. **Elevation drawing of a masking sound loudspeaker operation.**
(Courtesy Robert A. Hansen Associates, Inc.)

chapter ten

As Atlas supported the world on his shoulders, the office is supported by power — electric and telephone power at the work station. Bringing flexible and easily changed power capabilities to the open office is a design problem. People and machines move and tools change. Power and communication lines must follow people.

Hans Kreiks once proclaimed that wires are beautiful. The management of wires demands planning and design skills of great refinement. The visual chaos of wires that we see on the exterior, the proliferation of poles and power lines, are present in the interior as well, as we try to feed our power-hungry equipment with power from poles, floor outlets, wall outlets, and work station power sources.

We have a choice of bringing power through the ceiling or the floor. There are problems and limitations to both choices. The appearance of the floor-to-ceiling telephone and electric power pole still isn't satisfactory. Many floor fixtures are unsightly and create stumbling blocks. They are only considered if they can be hidden under desks. If the desk moves, there is an expensive relocation and scarred carpet. Virtually no design attention has been given to managing the machine appliance wires once we have provided the outlet.

Power and communications cables are quite different, both in function and design. They must be contained separately as the electrical code dictates but they can be utilized together.

FROM THE FLOOR

First, let us consider bringing power through the floor (Fig. 58). When it is possible to plan in the early stages of a building, accessibility and flexibility make the cellular raceway system one viable approach to bringing power to the open office. A second floor power system is the Sippican electrical floor assembly. A third system is that of the unlimited access of the raised floor.

Phone service, like electrical power, is a public utility and must be supplied to a building. Based on their past experience, the

A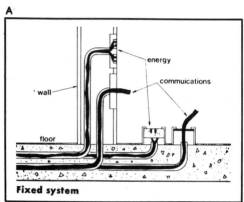

Fixed system

B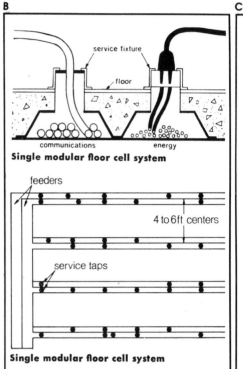

Single modular floor cell system

Single modular floor cell system

C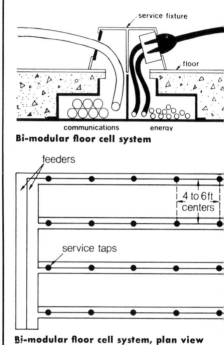

Bi-modular floor cell system

Bi-modular floor cell system, plan view

Fig. 58. **FLOOR POWER DISTRIBUTION SYSTEMS — FIXED CONDUIT SYSTEM.** A method, rather than a system, whereby an outlet or receptable is wired at a predetermined location. Any moves or changes require an additional circuit complete with metallic conduit or raceway. Essentially, changes require major modification to existing circuits. There is no pre-wiring facility incorporated in this type of approach. In the fixed system classification, two basic types are found — floor distribution and ceiling distribution. In either case, the distribution ends at a receptable on a wall or partition. The most common use of the fixed system is in small and older office buildings where electrical or telephone requirements are satisfied entirely by wall plugs or outlets. Extension of fixed systems into larger spaces is

accomplished by surface-mounted raceways placed either on the wall or directly on the floor. Addition of circuitry is usually difficult and expensive. Expense results from the necessity of adding new routing and raceways to create a new circuit. Very seldom can existing fixed-conduit systems accommodate new circuits, and, consequently, new circuits require new routing (A).

MODULAR SYSTEM. A system that can deliver an outlet or receptacle on a modular dimension. Most systems of this kind have raceways in place and can be wired when an outlet is required. The module usually established is between four to six feet. Sub-floor cells or raceways are an integral part of a concrete floor structure. A header or trenchway feeds a series of parallel cells. The

cells are located on 4- to 6-feet center lines. Because the cell system is an integral part of the building superstructure, capacity limitations are "built in." In early installations the cells were 1½ inches deep. They have increased to 3-inch and even to 5-inch depths to handle increases in circuitry. Initially developed to feed movable partitions, subfloor systems can also serve large spaces through a variety of floor fixtures. There are basically two variations of floor cells:

1. SINGLE MODULAR — Location of floor fixtures is available at any point along the cell run. Access is obtained by drilling a hole into the cell through the concrete (B).

2. BI-MODULAR — Floor fixture locations are predetermined by cell access fixtures located on the cell run on modules of 4- to 6-feet (C).

114

Bell Telephone Systems estimate that there is a need for one telephone in every 100 square feet in an open office. They established their Building Industry Consulting Service (BIC) in 1969 to help plan the integration of communications lines in new construction. They tried to design the maximum capacity to meet initial and future requirements, and they like to be consulted early in the planning of a facility. The Bell Systems prefer underfloor cellular grids and will help lay out the underfloor system to provide one telephone for every 100 square feet of usable space.

They plan the location of the apparatus closet and the main terminal, risers from floor to floor connecting with the apparatus closet, and the distribution system underfloor or ceiling. This places telephone service throughout the building so it can accommodate any design layout or change. The BIC service keeps all architectural plans on file to help with renovations and office expansion.

Within the cellular system are the electrical energy power lines as well (Fig. 59). The metal raceway grid embedded in the concrete floor has prepunched cells for access, either by using a concrete drill or where access inserts are set before the concrete is poured (Fig. 60). Some are activated for immediate use, others

Fig. 59. **Raceways carry lines from power closets through feeders or trenches which permit the routing and installation of 110V circuitry, telephone cables, closed circuit TV, CRT circuitry computer equipment cabling, and so on.**
(Courtesy H. H. Robertson Company)

Fig. 60. **Trench header and outlets being installed at Weyerhaeuser headquarters in Tacoma.**
(Courtesy H. H. Robertson Company)

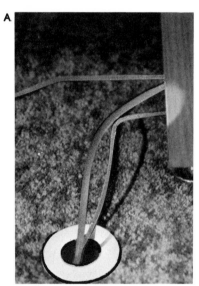

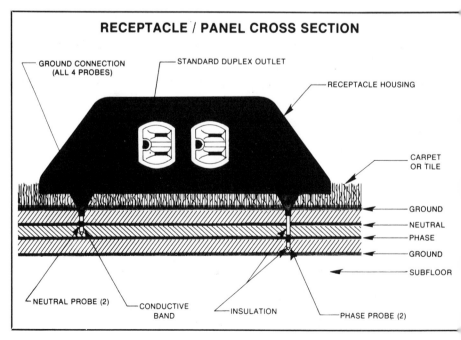

Fig. 61. **Activated outlets at Weyerhaeuser provide power, telephones and communications at desks and work stations. Each outlet serves 24 square feet of office area (A). Detail of unit at floor, completely flush with carpet. Weyerhaeuser has made over 1,000 outlet changes a year, activating previously unused locations and re-utilizing others (B).**
(Courtesy H. H. Robertson Company)

RECEPTACLE / PANEL CROSS SECTION

GROUND CONNECTION (ALL 4 PROBES)

STANDARD DUPLEX OUTLET

RECEPTACLE HOUSING

CARPET OR TILE

GROUND

NEUTRAL

PHASE

GROUND

SUBFLOOR

NEUTRAL PROBE (2)

CONDUCTIVE BAND

INSULATION

PHASE PROBE (2)

Fig. 62. **The Sippican Electrical Floor Assembly used modular panels to carry power and signals in a sandwich construction. The cross-section shows how the receptacle pierces the panel.**
(Courtesy Sippican)

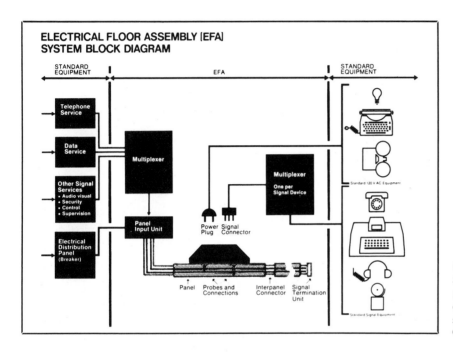

ELECTRICAL FLOOR ASSEMBLY (EFA)
SYSTEM BLOCK DIAGRAM

Fig. 63 **The interface between the Sippican system and the standard portions of a building's electrical and communications wiring is shown in this block diagram.** (Courtesy Sippican)

can be put into service as needed. When all the inserts are installed, flush with the carpet, they present a very acceptable appearance (Fig. 61), whether they are activated or not, unlike the ungainly junction boxes that are surface mounted and present such stumbling blocks. The system of flush mounted electrical telephone outlet floor boxes was first developed in Germany and used here at the Mercedes-Benz headquarters building. There they are installed five feet apart, the length of a table or desk, allowing for maximum flexibility.

The Sippican Electrical Floor Assembly (EFA) brings power to the open office in a completely different way. Power and communications are sandwiched in layers of wood (Fig. 62). The EFA system employs metallic sheets, not wires, as conductors. The sheets are layered under standard carpet throughout the office. Special outlet units or receptacles are placed wherever they are needed. They are easily relocated with a simple tool. There are no cables, cords, ducts, or poles involved (Fig. 63).

This innovative approach was encouraged by the General Services Administration. They installed it in a test area of 8,500 square feet in their Action Center in Washington, D.C. It is oper-

Fig. 64. **Raised Floors** — The raised or total-access floor systems were designed to provide infinite distribution capacity for computer rooms. The virtues of raised floors have influenced installations in office spaces where air, utilities, and wiring have unlimited distribution capability. Raised floors are installed on pedestals or jacks which suspend the floor 8 to 24 inches above a base floor. Modular panels, either covered with carpeting or vinyl tile, are placed on the pedestals. Access to electrical and telephone services is obtained through any selected panel. If change or relocation of service is required, the service panel can be relocated where desired. If new circuitry is required, the easily handled panel can be drilled, fixtures can be installed, and the panel can be replaced on the pedestal for wiring.

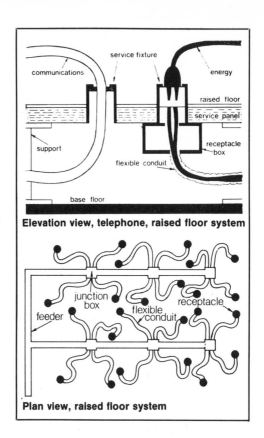

Elevation view, telephone, raised floor system

Plan view, raised floor system

ating in several other test areas but it is not being marketed yet until the settlement of an action pending with AT&T. At the GSA test installation, its assets, as well as its problems, were illustrated. It provides excellent overall power distribution but among the problems was the fact that up until now, it could only handle simple phones, not the more complex centrex phones. A separate raceway had to be provided for centrex switching.

The installation of this system was stalled forty-five days to identify who had jurisdiction since it had both telephone and electric power. The electric union finally prevailed. The concept and technology are innovative and it is anticipated that this technology will continue to develop.

The floor system, with unlimited access, is the elevated or raised floor (Fig. 64). It is built up over the concrete slab on little pedestals. It has become standard in computer installations because of the volume of cables and wires. Computers get very hot and the heat has to be drawn away. This floor lends itself to this situation as louvers can be built in so that air can be circulated around the computers and the heat drawn away. These floors can be used anywhere, even where there is no underfloor duct system, such as in older buildings.

Manufacturers of access floors envision lowering the now relatively high cost of this floor by eliminating concrete floor finishing and using the space to provide an HVAC type of system. These spaces can be available to provide plenum barriers to direct air as well as electrical and telephone systems and utilities, like piping, all with easy access. The Rouse Development in Columbia, Maryland, made use of these features with the Tate Access Floor System (Fig. 65).

Fig. 65. The Rouse Company in Columbia, Maryland, installed raised access floors throughout their headquarters building. The initial design concept was to use the ceiling as an unbroken, uncluttered plane, to reflect light rather than contain fixtures. The design concept affected every decision such as air distribution, acoustic control, and the design of panels and partitions. The poles and fixtures were developed to provide light, the raised floor panels are covered in carpet tiles in the office areas (above), and in teakwood parquet in the mail lobby (below).
(Courtesy Tate Industries)

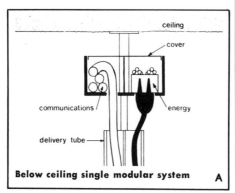

Below ceiling single modular system   A

ceiling
cover
communications
energy
delivery tube

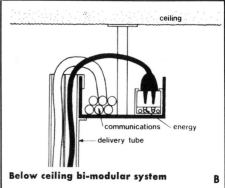

Below ceiling bi-modular system   B

ceiling
communications
energy
delivery tube

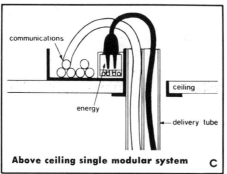

Above ceiling single modular system   C

communications
energy
ceiling
delivery tube

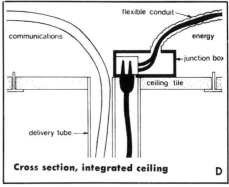

Cross section, integrated ceiling   D

flexible conduit
communications
energy
junction box
ceiling tile
delivery tube

Fig. 66. **Ceiling power distribution systems.** All above-and-below-ceiling systems investigated are designed to provide distribution to open-plan spaces where fixed and floor cell systems did not exist or were inadequate to meet the change rate within the office environment. Ceiling systems are secondary elements that can be expanded, changed, and modified without interfering with the primary structural elements of the building. In nearly every instance, wire and cable delivery from the ceiling is accomplished through metal tubes or channels that run from ceiling to floor or from ceiling to panel tops. There are three variations of modular ceiling systems:

1. BELOW-CEILING SINGLE MODULAR — parallel trays suspended below the ceiling on 4- to 6-foot centers. Access is available at any point along the tray (A).

2. BELOW-CEILING BI-MODULAR — parallel trays suspended below the ceiling on 4- to 6-foot centers. Access is available at points along the tray, usually on 4- to 6-foot centers (B).

3. ABOVE-CEILING SINGLE MODULAR — parallel trays located above suspended ceilings in such a way that delivery tubes can carry wires and cables to the floor through pre-determined points in the particular suspended ceiling (C).

The integrated ceiling sometimes offers flexibility factors similar to those found in raised floors. The space above the suspended ceiling is used for the routing of wires and cables. The simplest integrated ceiling consists of an exposed-grid, ceiling panel system. The panel is removable and can be relocated, with a delivery tube, at any place desired with the exception of where a lighting panel or air-conditioning vent panel is located. A more sophisticated integrated ceiling system can supply air, lighting, acoustical controls, electrical and telephone wiring raceways, and delivery tubes without, generally, conflicting with lighting or air vents in any desired location (D).

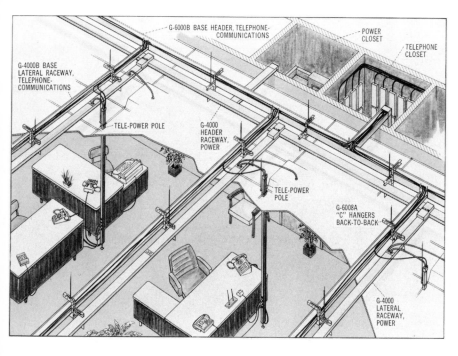

Fig. 67. **Ceiling channels bring power from the electrical and telephone closets to the power poles.**
(Courtesy The Wiremold Company)

FROM THE CEILING

Overhead ceiling spaces make it possible to bring electric and communications services to a point directly above the work station to be served. The power can be brought to the work station through outlets in partitions, poles, or flexible hoses (Fig. 66).

The greatest asset gained from bringing power from the ceiling sources is its easy accessibility. It is easier to reach wiring laying in raceways by pushing up a ceiling tile than it is going through carpet and cement to underfloor ducts (Fig. 67).

Ceiling systems maintain the same grid limitations that underfloor systems impose. The National Electric Code limits the use of metal conduit for electrical wiring to a six-foot length in ceiling spaces. This limits the service radius to six feet, similar to the five-foot grid used with underfloor duct systems. Telephone lines are kept in separate tandem raceways in the ceiling and they are serviced by the telephone company who brings them into a separate channel in the power pole. The electrical wire connects to the pole with the conduit. There are several designs and manufacturers of this kind of system. Among them 3M, Wiremold, Modulo-3, and Group Artec. Other manufacturers, like Hauserman, Westinghouse, and Herman Miller, bring cable and telephone lines from the ceiling to power panels that are part of complete work station furniture packages. Internal segmented

Fig. 68. **Telephone lines extend to a custom credenza in an informal conference area at the Arco headquarters in Los Angeles, California.**
(Courtesy Morganelli-Heumann and Associates)

compartments with separate raceways carry the power to outlets on the panel.

THROUGH THE FURNITURE

By having furniture that contains the wiring, an added extension of power lines becomes available (Fig. 68). Once the power and communication lines have left the ceiling or floor sources, they can be made to travel through multi-channel raceways in steel bases with access available on both sides of the raceways. They can run horizontally and link several work stations or they can run vertically to position telephone jacks and outlets at convenient levels, designed to conceal wiring under work surfaces or to be mounted on panels (Fig. 69 and 70). Among the manufacturers who have developed this facility are Knoll International, J. G. Sunar Systems, G. F. Equipment Company, and Steelcase.

Fig. 69. **The ability to handle electrical and telephone channels is designed into some furniture systems.**
(Courtesy Steelcase Inc.)

Fig. 70. **Wire management at the desk in concealed raceways accommodates the telephone and electrical needs of the user. The base of the pedestal can conceal the junction box.**
(Courtesy GF Equipment Company)

chapter eleven
design's
obligations

THE DESIGN PROCESS

Today, there is a general homogeneity of creative response. It seems to be a result of the way designers work in the relative anonymity of group effort. Designers respond to cultural trends through trade publications that have worldwide circulation. That helps to forumulate and institutionalize the styles and tastes of not only the design community, but also of the clients. In this relatively stable period designers are able to make some generalizations about where they have been and the nature of design today.

Designers today are part of the Bauhaus heritage, whose influence goes far beyond the creation of the international style. The Bauhaus established a rational analytic approach to design problems. Today the design process is based on the collection of data on which a solution is formed. Planning is part of the design process.

Space planning and design begins like every other design problem, whatever the project, with research and analysis. Michael Middleton said that when something comes about by design, it does not happen by chance. Design is a matter of preplanning, remote control, and method. It is the measure of a design's success that its aesthetic, functional, and material aspects are so completely fused that they cannot be isolated.

The requirements of the user are central to the design problem — not only the functional needs, but the social needs, as well. These are influenced by ideas about flexibility, systems thinking, and modular concepts.

Such specialization in our time has led to the rise in the number of managers engaged in planning, facilitating, and administering. As the nature of business changed, the owner-manager began to be replaced by an organizational structure with the capacity to delegate authority for decisions for a whole range of administrative tasks. The demands of business and organizational growth developed the specialist in administration and management, just as it developed specialists in other fields.

As the organization changes, so does the quality of life within corporations. They have to face the demands of a new breed of young employees. The young executive, as well as the managers and clerks, is looking for a quality of life not dependent on position, prestige, or salary alone.

One of the most controllable elements in a business lifestyle is the physical environment. In this post industrial society, perhaps designers see their role as fulfilling the needs of both the organization and of the work force. This would give the designer the role of the social agent, with a strong sense of moral obligation.

This obligation is not the same one that was felt in the forties and early fifties. At that time there was a vision of modern design as a means of improving the quality of contemporary life. These ideas were held widely and came in part from the concepts of the Bauhaus and in part from LeCorbusier's heritage of hope.

The idealism of social progress through design changed as the political climate under Senator Joseph McCarthy made it seem very naive. The promise of a better way of life through modern design will be slow to materialize, regardless of politics. Our sense of moral obligation now is defined by the user and the environment, not by social progress.

In this last chapter there are two obligations of design concern that will be discussed. The first concern is designing an environment that is barrier free. The second concern is the vital topic of life safety.

BARRIER-FREE DESIGN

Design research of user needs has largely overlooked an important segment of the population and has excluded them from the work place by creating architectural barriers. Imagine being faced with the problem of working after suffering an unexpected accident, a pulled muscle, or a bad back. If you are on crutches or have a brace or cane, you will find you cannot manage the revolving door, much less go up a few steps to an elevator bank. If you are in a wheelchair, the problems are compounded. These frustrations are felt by people recovering from surgery, cardiac conditions, or pregnancy, as well as those who are permanently disabled. We have inadvertently excluded the

The following are some potential barriers to the permanently and temporarily disabled, along with recommended antidotes:

POTENTIAL BARRIERS	RECOMMENDATIONS
Stairs leading to a building's entrance	At least one ground level entrance to the building.
Revolving doors	Avoid where possible.
Heavy doors	Where possible, replace with automatic doors.
Narrow doors	Make all doors at least 32" wide (to accommodate wheelchairs).
Corridors	Minimum 5' wide to permit passing.
Elevators	Elevators should be wide and deep enough to comfortably carry a person in a wheelchair. The "call" buttons should be a maximum of 3'6" above the floor.
Electrical outlets	Minimum of 18" above floor.
Room identification	Use raised letters for touch identification.
Drinking fountains	30" high.
Telephone booths	Telephone in wall with dial no more than 4' from the floor.
Highly polished floors	Nonslip surface.
Parking	Safe, reserved parking close to the entrance. A ramp rather than a curb should be near this parking area.
Rest rooms	One properly equipped toilet stall should be provided for the handicapped in all public rest rooms.

Table 19. **POTENTIAL BARRIERS AND RECOMMENDED ANTIDOTES**

physically handicapped from the work place. Most buildings and offices are designed for the physically able. Architectural barriers exist in these spaces, making it almost impossible for a handicapped person to work in them. These barriers create a feeling of total helplessness. We need to create barrier-free environments.

Barrier-free implies a lack of obstacles. Our intent should be to have buildings that may be entered and used by all. These barriers include steps and revolving doors or narrow doors. Once inside the entrance, a person in a wheelchair, on crutches or using a cane must be able to move with ease and independence. An estimated ten percent of our population is affected by this problem. It is not confined to those who have permanent impairments. There is no clearly defined separation between who is physically able and who is handicapped until the problem arises. Here is a list of potential barriers and recommendations (Table 19).

Federal legislation requires that public structures, as well as those financially assisted with Federal funds, be made accessible to the handicapped. The law also stipulates when public structures undergo extensive alterations the elimination of barriers to the handicapped shall be included as part of the contract. These buildings can then display the internationally

Fig. 71. **The international symbol of access.**

accepted seal, "the symbol of access," indicating that access is available to all (Fig. 71). About forty states have similar measures. Some states, like New Jersey, are adopting building codes affecting all private projects as well.

A comprehensive barrier-free design standard that updates and includes input from many sources was prepared for the New Jersey Easter Seal Society in 1975. It should be referred to for definitive specifications and up-to-date information. For further reference, the American Institute of Architects published an annotated bibliography on barrier-free architecture in the A.I.A. Journal in March 1969. It includes several international references.

LIFE SAFETY

A roaring fire swept through ten floors of the World Trade Center in February 1975. There have been very few spectacular fires in the fifty years between 1917 and 1967 and almost no loss of live. The fires during this period were serious but they were controlled. This remarkable record changed dramatically after 1968. Since then there have been a series of major fires that involved many fatalities. New hazards exist that are a danger to life.

What was the cause of this change? There were high-rise office buildings in New York City for 100 years that didn't present any unusual hazards. Primarily, it is because of the use of highly combustible materials, the spread of fire through central air conditioning, faults in design, and the hazards of wiring.

Combustible material such as highly flammable foamed polyurethane and foam rubber cushioning burn at an extremely high rate, releasing flammable gases and noxious smoke. This material burns very rapidly and ignites other combustibles so that fire spreads with great speed.

The fire that swept through ten floors of the World Trade Center was started by an arsonist who ignited a sofa in an executive office of the R.J. Saunders Company on the eleventh floor (Fig. 72). The cushion burned fast and gave off tremendous quanti-

Fig. 72. **Fire at the World Trade Center started in the 11th floor offices of R. J. Saunders. This photograph, taken just after the fire, shows the total destruction of the area. The file room is at the left. The fire started in an office on the right.** (Courtesy W. R. Powers, N. Y. Board of Fire Underwriters)

ties of smoke and heat. Moments after the alarm had been given, police found the door to the offices too hot to open. A file room where all the records were exposed and a gallon of duplicating fluid, methyl alcohol, were set aflame by the heat. Telephone cables insulated with polyethylene and polyvinyl chloride ignited and spread the fire vertically through telephone closets from the ninth to the nineteenth floor.

The heat was so intense on the eleventh floor that the ceiling

Fig. 73. Telephone cables passing through an opening in the closet floor. The original fire-damaged cables have been replaced. Note the spalling concrete. Holes in the closet walls allowed the fire to enter and spread to other telephone closets vertically. These openings were not fire stopped in the North Tower.
(Courtesy W. R. Powers, N. Y. Board of Fire Underwriters)

gave way after less than an hour. The steel decking in the cellular floor got so hot that it ignited the telephone cables that were lying in cells above.

The World Trade Center is unique in many aspects but it has much in common with other high-rise office buildings everywhere. A spreading fire is carried throughout a building and intensifies as it goes through the central air conditioning system. Air conditioning is not a hazard, it is an instrumentality that enters into the fire problem. Design faults that lead to openings in fire-rated floors or walls are avenues for the heat and gases to travel, spreading the fire (Fig. 73).

Telephone cables can carry fire through a wall. While an individual cable is hard to ignite, a bundle of them lying parallel act like logs in a fireplace and will burn intensely with the fire traveling throughout a.building. A substantial number of fires of electrical origin have occurred in telephone equipment.

Building codes regulate exit requirements, distances to exits, sprinklers, stand pipes, and flame-spread ratings on interior finishes. The National Bureau of Standards and the Model Building Codes are studying the potential fire hazards from foam and plastics, but, as yet, no standards have emerged from this research. At present, there are some 300 to 400 different flammability standards in use by various Federal Government Agencies, State municipalities, and specifiers. This proliferation of standards has created unrealistic conditions for anyone trying to evolve a safe interior environment.

All of these conditions can be controlled with the installation of automatic sprinklers. "The use of sprinklers is the best way to return building protection to the level of the past," is the unequivocal opinion of W. Robert Powers of the New York Board of Fire Underwriters. Where that is not possible, New York City has provided that high-rise office buildings conform to a group of regulations known as Local Law No. 5.

Designers and owners or tenants must provide an inherently safe building and minimize the effects of a fire. Where highly combustible materials are used or are present, sprinklers should be provided. When that is done, practically any other precautions that have to be taken for the sake of getting people out can be eliminated. A sprinkler system is sufficient to control the spread of flames and to insure life safety. Its success ratio is very high.

The fire at the World Trade Center occurred late at night after 11:30 p.m. What would its effects have been if people had been working there? During each day in one tower, there are 50,000 working people and 65,000 visitors. When a fire breaks out, there is no way to evacuate people quickly. Ironically, in spite of this, the World Trade Center is considered among the safest buildings in New York City by the New York Board of Fire Underwriters. This is because of two unique fire safety features. The Port Authority placed limits on the flammability of contents and they established a fire safety plan.

Even before the first tenants moved in, the Port Authority de-

Fig. 74. **Control panel at the World Trade Center, Police headquarters. Fire alarms are received here and are transmitted to the Fire Department via an alarm box or by "hot line" telephone.**
(Courtesy W. R. Powers, N. Y. Board of Fire Underwriters)

veloped stringent specifications for the flammability of furnishings and urged their use by their tenants. These recommendations do not call for completely noncombustible furnishings but they do limit the fire hazard to prevent extremely rapid combustion. If tenants supported these recommendations, the chances of a serious fire would be small. The Port Authority's fire-safety program has a fire-fighting unit that communicates with tenants and aids in evacuation (Fig. 74). Fire drills are held every three months with the tenants. Of prime importance is the fire drill held every month with the New York City Fire Department to insure that its personnel are familiar with the building layout, stairs, elevators, and soon, to be able to handle a real fire emergency.

Fire safety is life safety. Designers have the responsibility and the obligation to minimize hazards. This can be done by limiting the combustibility of furnishings and having evacuation plans, but most effective of all is the presence of automatic sprinklers to create an inherently safe building.

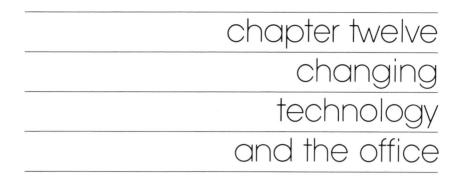

chapter twelve

changing

technology

and the office

Looking back over fifty years, we can see the vast impact technological changes have had on the office (Fig. 75). The work that is done in the office remains basically unchanged. What has changed is as a result of the tools that are in use. Changes in technology have transformed the office.

Although the six shirt-sleeved white-collar men we see in the photograph had one telephone, incandescent light, and undoubtedly a manual typewriter, we see the inkwells on each desk and the pen poised over one ear. The busy scribes at their desks seem to place the office on Tuesday, September 15, 1925, closer to the Nineteenth Century than to the office of today. Most of the work done in the open office shown in the photograph seems based on handwritten records and correspondence.

As specialized machines were introduced into general office use, writing, calculating, and communications were transformed and so was the office. Just as speed and efficiency were the classic factors in the factory assembly line, technology was changing the office as well. In Chapter VII, the office was described as a word processing factory. The transformation from handwritten correspondence to computerized word processing started with the first typewriter.

THE TYPEWRITER

The typewriter, which has virtually eliminated handwritten correspondence and recordkeeping, appeared about one hundred years ago. This common office machine revolutionized office procedures and was the forerunner of all other key-driven machines.

The records of the British Patent Office show that the first patent for a typewriter was granted in 1714. It was not until 1868 that a practical, working model was developed (Fig. 76). E. Remington and Sons, Gunsmiths, tried to market one without too much success. One problem was the lack of competent operators. This led to the development of the modern commercial school which opened the doors to business for young women.

Fig. 75. **A busy office, September 15, 1925.**
(Courtesy of Sperry-Remington)

Left:
Fig. 76. **An early manual typewriter, 1876.**
(Courtesy of Sperry-Remington)

Right:
Fig. 77. **One of the first electric typewriters, 1925.**
(Courtesy of Sperry-Remington)

Opposite:
Fig. 78. **Magnetic automatic typewriter.**
(Courtesy of I.B.M.)

Many improvements have been made in the typewriter since its invention, the most important being the electric typewriter (Fig. 77) and the magnetic automatic typewriter (Fig. 78). The electric typewriter was first developed by Thomas Edison in 1872 but this evolved into the ticker-tape printer. It was not until 1920 that a working electric typewriter was developed. The typewriter has spawned many offspring beside the ticker-tape printer. It has been developed into accounting machines that have a place in data processing and computer use. Keyboard terminals designed for data input, using a common language, characterize a wide variety of machines that can be tied together, such as typewriters, calculating machines, printing telegraphs, data processing computers, and electronic storage systems and composing and automatic remote control typewriters. High-speed printing machines were introduced in 1953.

The stenographic process has also been accelerated. The time-honored method of dictation in which a stenographer writes in shorthand for later transcription demanded skill and a high level of accuracy, especially when there was a delay in transcription and memory could not serve. New dictating machines have an easy advantage over Gregg's Shorthand and almost eliminate the need for the presence of a stenographer. Dictating and transcribing machines have increased typing efficiency and created better work flow.

Carbon paper has transformed the typewriter into a duplicating machine but the number of legible copies one typist can make at a time is extremely limited. Carbon copies never look like the original and would be limited to about eight on a manual typewriter and about eighteen on an electric typewriter. The stencil method of duplication could produce up to 5,000 copies and offset duplication offers mass production. Now, photocopying and microfilm reproduction are readily available for office use. Xerography, a dry electrical process based on magnetic principles, will reproduce unlimited copies that may be enlarged, reduced, and collated. Another device for high-speed reproduction is the use of text editors and automatic remote control typewriters. Text editors record all key strokes on a magnetic tape and can "play" them back when the text is in finished form. Word processing or editing typewriters were pioneered in the early 1960's by IBM. A sheet of paper can automatically be typed back completely corrected at the rate of 150 words per minute. Changes can be made by magnetic erasing and additions may be automatically inserted as if they had been typed in the beginning. This type of repetitive typing is used for insurance form letters and contract documents. One example of the application is at the Colonial Penn Group where five secretaries use a system that can turn out 3,000 form letters a day. Other users find that output varies with the situation.

Fig. 79. **An abacus — the Greek word for the counting board,** abax, **may have had derived from the Hebrew** abaq **meaning dust. The early counting boards were covered by a thin layer of dust or sand on which the numerals could be traced with the finger or stylus.**
(Courtesy of I.B.M.)

Fig. 80. **Blaise Pascal, 17th century mathematician and inventor of the first digital calculator.**
(Courtesy of I.B.M.)

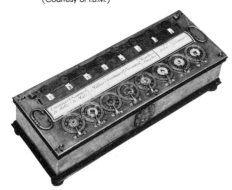

Fig. 81. **Pascal's calculator, developed in 1642.**

CALCULATORS AND COMPUTERS

The history of computers must start with the basic tool, the abacus (Fig. 79). Developed possibly in 2000 B.C., it was not until the Age of Reason in seventeenth-century Europe that a thrust of intellectual creativity developed the need for a digital calculator. The great rise of interest in the natural world and the developing theories of physics of Galileo, Kepler, Descartes, and Newton called for substantial calculations. The French scientist and writer, Blaise Pascal's fascination for mathematics, led him to develop a theory of probability and, at the age of nineteen in 1642, he invented the first digital calculator (Figs. 80 and 81). Leibniz (Fig. 82) invented the multiplying calculator (Fig. 83) in 1671 but it was not until the nineteenth century that the desk calculator was in use. These machines were mechanical and the time required for calculation depended upon the speed of the user (Fig. 84). Vannevar Bush and his associates at M.I.T. developed the first differential analyzer in 1930. This made it possible to do complex mathematical calculations. It was an automatic calculator that could be programmed to different types of problems and was the forerunner of today's electronic high-speed computer.

The development of a machine that could do complex calculations and print out the results developed from an early jacquard automatic weaving loom of 1800 (Fig. 85) that was operated from instructions on punched cards. Then, in the early 1800's, this principle was applied by Charles Babbage and was developed by Hollerith (Fig. 86) into a mechanical device for tabulating the U.S. Census in 1890 (Fig. 87). It was then applied to the New York Central's freight car accounting system and adapted to the needs of insurance companies.

Scientists developing new weaponry in World War II needed new ways to handle the mountains of data they were generating. Machines were developed, using vacuum tubes. This produced a radical change in terms of speed, flexibility, and function in machines. The slow movement of switches in electrically driven mechanical equipment was replaced by the swift motion of electrons. The result was that the speed of calculation was increased a thousand times.

Fig. 83. **The Leibniz calculator, 1671.**
(Courtesy of I.B.M.)

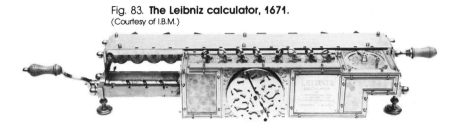

Fig. 82. **Gottfried Wilhelm Leibniz, German philosopher and a major systematic thinker of modern times.**
(Courtesy of I.B.M.)

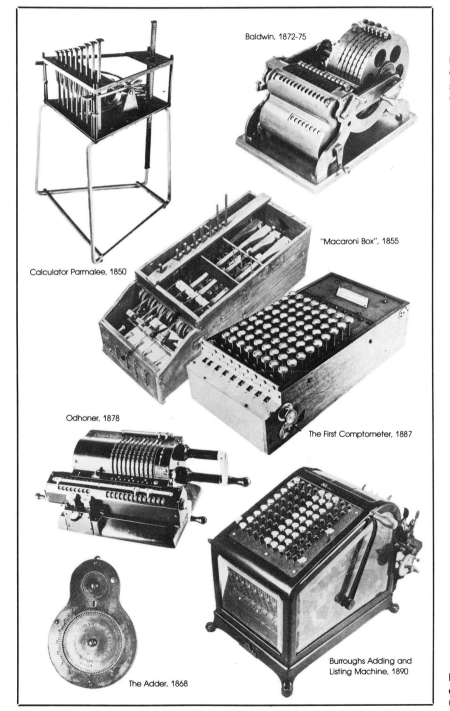

Baldwin, 1872-75

"Macaroni Box", 1855

Calculator Parmalee, 1850

Odhoner, 1878

The First Comptometer, 1887

The Adder, 1868

Burroughs Adding and Listing Machine, 1890

Fig. 84. **Highlights in history of the calculator.**
(Courtesy of I.B.M.)

139

Fig. 88. **A magnetic character reader.**
(Courtesy of I.B.M.)

Fig. 85. **The Jacquard loom operated with punch cards that controlled the weaving pattern.**
(Courtesy of I.B.M.)

Fig. 86. **Hollerith's mechanical tabulating machine.**
(Courtesy of I.B.M.)

IBM's first automatic digital computer was completed in 1944. The first large scale system was introduced in 1952 and was used by a small number of scientists and engineers. The third generation of computers of the 60's was vastly improved and added peripheral equipment such as graphic display units and optical scanners.

Supplementing the information system of computers is the use of microfilm technology, coupled with video transmission. This has made possible the transmission of vast amounts of information by cathode ray tubes, coaxial cable, or microwave. Terminals everywhere in the country can have the latest information available in seconds. It has been put to good use by airlines to reduce its maintenance manuals and parts catalog and to update them easily anywhere in the world.

The growth of the banking industry in the 60's meant that data required to operate also grew at a staggering rate. The development of magnetic character sensing devices (Fig. 88) made it possible to cope with over twenty billion checks which circulate annually in the United States. Previously, a check was handled six times before it was cancelled and returned. Magnetic devices now permit the data to be read directly and has permitted growth without staggering costs.

The future of the banking industry will be strongly influenced when electronic funds transfer (E.F.T.) becomes widespread, probably by 1980. This will link banks directly with the Federal Reserve and operate like a credit card system. Funds are transferred with no actual exchange of money. A pilot program, now being tried, sends social security checks directly to a recipient's bank rather than to his or her home. It could be extended to the transfer of paychecks, eliminating payroll departments. Financial institutions may do that work in the future, handling all deductions, loan payments, as well as all the usual banking services with no actual exchange of funds.

Fig. 87. **Scientific American, August 30, 1890, reports on the use of the Hollerith tabulator for the United States Census.**
(Courtesy of I.B.M.)

Fig. 89. **Since the development of the first experimental model in 1975, the telephone has taken many shapes.**

Left:
The historic model of 1876. The receiver was a tuned reed.

Center:
The wall set was developed in 1878 and added a new feature, a second wooden transmitter-receiver, you could use either for talking or listening. The crank generated power to signal the operator.

Right:
The desk set of 1892 was more compact and decorative.

THE TELEPHONE

The amazing telephone, our lifeline of communication, seems absolutely indispensable to modern life. From that day in 1876 when Alexander Graham Bell transmitted the famous lines "Mr. Watson, come here, I want you" and founded the telephone business in 1878, it quickly became an indispensable tool (Fig. 89). In the beginning of the 1960's, there were 130 billion telephones in the world and 55 percent of them were in the United States. Washington, D.C. had more phones with 71.4 per hundred population than any other city in the world. There is no indication of saturation in the demand for phones. Telephone service can be adapted to provide other types of communications as well. The earliest use of telephone lines was to relate telegraph messages. As many as eighteen telegraph channels can be transmitted in one telephone circuit. The channels can serve both telephone and telegraph services and are used extensively by industry, finance, the press, and government. Tele-

Above left:
The first commercial telephone, 1877, was used by a Boston banker who leased two units and attached a line between his home and his office.

Right:
The first dial telephone, 1919.

Below left:
The desk set of 1930 came with or without a dial.

(Courtesy of the American Telephone and Telegraph Companies)

phone circuits are also used to transmit pictures satisfactorily. In the 1940's, the development of coaxial cables and radio relay made transmission of intercity TV practical.

The development of the transistor foreshadowed various changes. Because of the transistor's low-power dissipation and low-voltage requirement, other electronic components associated with it can be miniaturized. The new art of solid state electronics provided the basis for the changes in both switching and transmission technology. Research into the development of extremely wide bands of frequency will provide a great multiplicity of communication channels of increasing importance to world communication. Experiments with radio communications via satellite offer potentials for wide transmission bands used for TV, telephone, and other data communications across oceans. In 1915, the first transcontinental telephone line was opened between New York and San Francisco. In 1927, New York and London were joined by radio telephone, and in 1956, the first undersea telephone cable was laid in the North Atlantic. Subsequently, other cables link the United States with Alaska and Hawaii.

Applewhite, Philip B., *Organizational Behavior*, Prentice Hall Inc., 1965.

Bach, Fred W., "A Systems Approach to Ergonomics," *Modern Office Procedures*, October, 1974.

Barnet, Robert, and Ronald Muller, "A Reporter at Large (Multinational Corporations — Part II)," *New Yorker*, December 9, 1974, pp. 100–160.

Barron, Maurice, "Computers: New Decision Making Tools for Managing the Professional Office," *Progressive Architecture*, July, 1971, pp. 76–77.

Bass, Alan M., "Systems Building Technics," *Analysis and Bibliography Series*, No. 15, ERIC Clearinghouse on Educational Management, July, 1972.

Bazjanac, Vladimir, "Computer Simulation: A Realistic Assessment," *Progressive Architecture*, July, 1971, pp. 80–82.

Bensman, Joseph, and Arthur J. Vidich, *The New American Society — The Revolution of the Middle Class*, Quadrangle Books, Chicago, Illinois, 1971.

Bergeron, Lionel L., "The Word Processing Survey," *Management Review*, July 1975, condensed from *Journal of Systems Management*, March, 1975, pp. 47–50.

Boje, Axel, Ed., *Open Plan Offices*, B. H. Wolley, Business Books Ltd., London, England, 1971.

Brett, Lionel, *The World of Architecture*, Thomas Nelson Sons Ltd., London, England, 1963.

Brill, Michael, Terry Collison, and Eileen Harvard, *The Management of Change and Productive Interiors*, Prepared by the Buffalo Organization for Social and Technological Innovation, Inc. for Hauserman, Inc., 1972.

Buckley, Mary and David Baum, *Color Theory*, Gale Research, Book Tower, Detroit, Michigan, 1975.

Chambers, Harry T., *Office Planning for Profit*, Business Books Ltd., London, England, 1972.

Christensen, Jean, "Why Credit Unions Bought a Bank — A move into Electronic Transfers of Money," *New York Times,* January 12, 1975

Coniglio, Cheryl, "How to Evaluate User Needs," *Designer Magazine*, September, 1975, p. 22.

Corbin, Len, "Task Lighting Sources in Furniture Save Energy in Growing Power Crunch," *Contract Magazine*, March, 1974.

Crouch, C. L., "Can We Scientifically Bridge the Gap Between the Architect and the Illuminating Engineer," *Lighting Design and Application*, November, 1972, pp. 38–43.

Diffrient, Niels, Alvin R. Tilley, and Joan Bardagiy, *Hunanscale 1/2/3*, M.I.T. Press, 1975.

Drucker, Peter F., *Management: Tasks, Responsibilities, Practices*, Harper and Row, New York, 1973.

Dufy, Frank, *New Approach to Office Planning — An Anbar Monograph*, Anbar Publications Ltd., London, 1969.

Eberhard, John P., "A Humanist Case for the Systems Approach," *A.I.A. Journal*, July, 1968, pp. 34–38.

Ehrenkrantz, Ezra D., A.I.A., "The System to Systems," *A.I.A. Journal*, May, 1970, pp. 56--59.

Ewing, David W., *The Human Side of Planning, Tool or Tyrant*, Macmillan Co., New York, 1969.

Fisher, Harrison, *Business Machines*, American Technical Society, Chicago, Illinois, 1959.

Flowers, Vincent S., "Managerial Values for Working," American Management Association's *A.M.A. Survey Report*, 1975.

Forrest, Gordon, "The Office Environmental Planning," Commissioned by the Office of Design, Department of Industry, Trade and Commerce, Ottowa, Canada for the National Design Council, 1970.

Frampton, Kenneth, "Transformation of the Interior," *Progressive Architecture*, November, 1973, p. 110.

Freedman, Jonathan, *Crowding and Behavior, the Psychology of High Density Living*, The Viking Press, New York,

Freedman, Jonathan L., "No, Actually Crowding Isn't Bad." *The New York Times*, October 15, 1974.

Friedman, John, *Retracking America: A Theory of Transactive Planning*, Anchor Press/Doubleday, Garden City, New York, 1973.

Friedmann, Arnold, John F. Pile, and Forrest Wilson, *Interior Design, An Introduction to Architectural Interiors*, American Elsevier Inc., New York, 1970.

Gleason, Robert W., Ed. *The Essential Pascal*, Mentor Omega Books, New York, 1966.

Goldstein, Seth, "Automating the Typing Pool," *Dunn's*, April, 1973.

Goodwin, Richard N., "Awaiting the Copernican Question," *The New Yorker*, January 6, 1975, pp. 38–49.

Greenberg, Donald P., "Computer Graphics in Architecture," *Scientific American*, May, 1974, pp. 98–106.

Griffin, William V., Joseph H. Mauritzen, and Joyce V. Kasmar, "The Psychological Aspects of the Architectural

Environment: A Review," *American Journal of Psychiatry*, February, 1969, pp. 93–98.

Guarra, Francisco, "The Use of Random in Architectural Design," *Bulletin of Computer Aided Architecture Design*, No. 14, January, 1974.

Gueft, Olga, "Designs for Business, Inc.", *Interiors*, Jan. 1960, pp. 72–99, pp. 141–154.

Haines, Richard F., "Color Design for Habitability," Proceedings of the 28th Annual Conference, California Council, A.I.A., Monterey, California, November 24, 1973.

Hall, Edward T., "A System for the Notation of Proxemic Behavior," *American Anthropologist*, Vol. 165, 1963, pp. 1003–1026.

Hall, Edward T., *The Hidden Dimension*, Doubleday, New York, 1966.

Hall, Edward T., *The Silent Language*, Doubleday, New York, 1959.

Handler, A. Benjamin, *Systems Approach to Architecture*, American Elsevier Publishing Company Inc., New York, 1970.

Hare, A. Paul, "Dimensions of Social Interaction," *Behavior Sciences*, Vol. 5, 1960, pp. 211–215.

Harper, A. Neil, Ed. *Computer Applications in Architecture and Engineering*, McGraw Hill, 1968.

Helson, H., and T. Landsford, "The Role of Spectral Energy of Source and Background Color in the Pleasantness of Object Colors," *Applied Optics*, Vol. 9, No. 7, July, 1970, pp. 1513–1562.

Herzberg, Frederick, *The Motivation to Work*, Wiley, New York, 1959.

Herzberg, Frederick, *Work and the Nature of Man*, World, New York, 1966.

Hilbertz, Wolf, "Towards Cybertecture," *Progressive Architecture*, April, 1970, p. 98.

Horowitz, Harold, "The Program's the Thing," *A.I.A. Journal*, May, 1967, pp. 94–100.

Jacobs, Herman S., "Executive Productivity," American Management Association's *A.M.A. Survey Report*, 1974.

Jacobs, Jane, *The Death and Life of Great American Cities*, Vintage Books, New York, 1961.

Kaplan, Archie, "The Significance of Anthropometrics," *Industrial Design Magazine*, November-December, 1975, pp. 51–53.

Kepes, Gyorgy, *Language of Vision*, Paul Theobald, Chicago, Illinois, 1944.

Kleeman, Walter, Jr., "How to Establish Office Distance: 66 Inches or 6,600 Miles," *Contract Magazine*, August, 1971, pp. 80–83.

Kleeman, Walter, Jr., *Interior Ergonomics — Significant*

Dimensions in Interior Design and Planning: A Selected Bibliography, Council of Planning Librarians, Monticello, Illinois, 1972.

Kleinschrod, Walter A., *Word Processing*, American Management Association, New York, 1974.

Kroemer, K. H. Eberhard, and Joan C. Robinette, "Ergonomics in the Design of Office Furniture — A Review of European Literature." Aerospace Medical Research Laboratories, Wright-Patterson Air Force Base, Ohio, 1968.

Le Breton, Preston P., *General Administration: Planning and Implementation*. Holt, Rinehart and Winston, 1965.

Lippet, Ronald, *The Dynamics of Planned Change*, Harcourt, Brace, and World, New York, 1958.

Little, Kenneth B., "Personal Space," *Journal of Experimental Social Psychology*, Vol. 1, 1965, pp. 237–247.

Mach, Ruth P., *Planning on Uncertainty, Decision Making in Business and Government Administration*, Wiley Interscience Sons Inc., New York, 1971.

Maslow, Abraham H., *Motivation and Personality*, Harper and Row, New York, 1959.

Meyers, M. Scott, and Susan Meyers, "Toward Understanding the Changing Work Ethic," *California Management Review*, Spring, 1974.

Middleton, Michael, *Group Practice in Design*, George Braziller Inc., New York, 1969.

Miller, David W., and Starr Martink, *The Structure of Human Decisions*, Prentice Hall, Englewood Cliffs, New Jersey, 1967.

Mills, Edward D., *The Changing Workplace, Modern Technology and the WORKING Environment*, George Godwin Ltd., London, England, 1972.

Milne, Murray, Ed., *Computer Graphics in Architecture and Design*, Yale University School of Art and Architecture, 1969.

Milne, Murray, "From Pencil Points to Computer Graphics," *Progressive Architecture*, June, 1970, pp. 168–177.

Mintz, David A., "The Role of the Lighting Consultant," *Interiors Magazine*, December, 1974, pp. 94–97.

Mintzberg, Henry, "Making Manaement Information Useful," *Management Review*, May, 1975, pp. 34–38, condensed from "Impediments to the Use of Management Information," The National Association of Accountants, 1975.

Mogulescu, Maurice, *Profit through Design Rx for Effective Office Space Planning*, American Management Association, New York, 1970.

Murrell, K. F. H., *Ergonomics: Man in His Working Environment*, Chapman & Hull, London, England, 1965

Nowlis, David P., Ph.D., "Freedom, Dignity and the Measure of Habitability," Proceedings of the 28th Annual

Conference, California Council, A.I.A., Monterey, California, November 24, 1973.

Ostrander, Edward R., "The Competitive Edge," *Designer Magazine*, September, 1975, pp. 4–5.

Payne, Bruce, *Planning for Company Growth — The Executive's Guide to Effective Long Range Planning*, McGraw Hill, New York, 1963.

Payne, Stanley L., *The Art of Asking Questions*, Princeton University Press, Princeton, N. J., 1951.

Perin, Constance, *With Man in Mind: An interdisciplinary Prospectus for Environmental Design*, The M.I.T. Press, Cambridge, Mass., 1970.

Pilditch, James, *Communications by Design, a Study in Corporate Identity*, McGraw Hill, England, 1970.

Pile, John, Ed., *Interiors Second Book of Offices*, Whitney Library of Design, New York, 1969.

Porte, P. C. Andre de la, "Group Norms: Key to Building a Winning Team," *Personnel Magazine*, September-October, 1974. pp. 60–67.

Propst, Robert L., "Process Aesthetic: Some Thoughts on the Thinking Process," *Progressive Architecture*, November, 1974 p. 78.

Propst, Robert L., *The Office, A Facility Based on Change*, The Business Press, Elmhurst, Illinois, 1968.

Rapp, Donald G., and Dan D. Drew, "Computer Planning the Community College," *Progressive Architecture*, September, 1971, pp. 78–79.

Rasmussen, Steen Eiler, *Experiencing Architecture*, The M.I.T. Press, Cambridge, Mass., 1959.

Reichman, Walter, and Marguerite Levy, "Psychological Restraints on Effective Planning," *Management Review*, October, 1975, pp. 37–42.

Reif, Rita, "Word Processing Comes of Age," *New York Times*, Sunday, May 4, 1975.

Ripnen, Kenneth H., R.A., A.I.A., *Office Building and Office Layout Planning*, McGraw Hill, New York, 1960.

Rogers, Jon, Ph.D., "Environmental Needs of Individuals and Groups," Proceedings of the 28th Annual Conference, California Council, A.I.A., Monterey, California, November 24, 1973.

Saphier, Michael, *Office Planning and Design*, McGraw Hill, New York, 1968.

Schiff, Robert A., "Satellite Administrative Zones", *Information and Records Management*, Feb. 1972, pp. 10–12.

Schutte, Thomas F., *The Uneasy Coalition — Design in Corporate America*, University of Pennsylvania Press, Philadelphia, Pennsylvania, 1975.

Senger, John, "Systematic Problem Solving vs. Creativity — What's the Difference?" *Management Review*, March, 1975, pp. 54–57, condensed from "Organizational Problem Solving and Creativity," *Public Personnel Management*, November–December, 1974.

Shoshkes, Lila, *Contract Carpeting, A Critical Guide To Specification and Performance for Architects and Designers*, Whitney Library of Design, Watson Guptill, New York, 1974.

Sloan, Sam A., "Designs Influenced by Psycho-Social Factors Result in Happier, More Productive Employees," *Contract Magazine*, August, 1972, pp. 80–83.

Smith, C. Ray, "Editorial", *Interiors*, Sept. 1975, p. 87.

Sommer, Robert, *The Ecology of Study Areas*, University of California, Davis, California, 1968.

Sommer, Robert, *Design Awareness*, Rinehart Press, San Francisco, California, 1972.

Sommer, Robert, *Personal Space: The Behavioral Basis of Design*, Prentice-Hall, Inc., Englewood Cliffs, N.J. 1969.

Sommer, Robert, *Tight Spaces, Hard Architecture and How to Humanize It*, Prentice-Hall, Inc., Englewood Cliffs, N.J., 1975.

Spiro, Kornel, "Computer Systems of the Future," *Management Review*, April, 175, pp. 23–31.

Stainbrook, E., "Architects Not only Design Hospitals, They also Design Patient Behavior," *Modern Hospital*, Vol 106, p. 100, 1966.

Steele, Fred I., *Physical Settings and Organizational Development*, Addison-Wesley Publishing Co., Reading, Mass., 1973.

Stewart, Clifford D., and Lee Kaiman, "Can a 54 Year Old Architectural Firm Find Romance and Happiness With an Interactive Computer System?" *Progressive Architecture*, July, 1971, p. 64.

Stonebraker, Gary K., and Staff of the Advanced Planning Research Group, Inc., "Computers and School Planning," Prepared for the Educational Facilities Lab., New York, 1968.

Terkel, Studs, *Working*, Pantheon Press, New York, 1974.

Wilson, Forrest, "The Education of an Interior Designer," *Progressive Architecture*, November, 1973, pp. 122–123.

Yee, Rodger, "The Invisible Architects, *Progressive Architecture*, October, 1974, pp. 106–108.

"A Home in Business for the Radical Generations," *Business Week*, October 5, 1974.

A Modern Consciousness — D. J. De Pree and Florence Knoll, Published for the National Collection of Fine Arts by the Smithsonian Institution Press, Washington, D.C., 1975.

An Annotated Bibliography on Barrier-Free Architecture, *A.I.A. Journal*, The American Institute of Architects, March, 1969, pp. 49–50, 82–84.

Annual Report — 1974, Illuminating Engineering Research Institute.

"An Overview of Word Processing: How IBM sees the Basic Concept of Word Processing and How It can Work for *Any* Company!" A Dartnell Office Administration Service Report.

A Proposed Barrier-Free Design Standard, Submitted by the New Jersey Easter Seal Society, Ad Hoc Committee on Barrier-Free Design, March 3, 1975.

"Architecture for Human Behavior," Collected Papers from a Mini-Conference, Philadelphia Chapter of The American Institute of Architecture, 1971.

"Are You Ready for the Telecommunications Revolution? *Industry Week*, July 8, 1974.

Carpet Specifiers Handbook, The Carpet and Rug Institute, Dalton, Georgia, 1974.

"Chair Design Requirements Start With Human Dimensions," *Contract Magazine*, August, 1975, pp. 52–55.

Color and Light, General Electric Company, Large Lump Department, Nela Park, Cleveland, Ohio, 1974.

"Designer's Utopia?" (Staff Article), *Progressive Architecture*, July, 1971, pp. 84–88.

Effective Seeing in an Era of Energy Conservation — A Review of Institute Findings, Illuminating Engineering Research Institue.

"Establishing the Program," (Staff Article), *Progressive Architecture*, January, 1974, p. 82.

Guide for Acoustical Performance Specification of an Integrated Ceiling and Background System, General Service Administration, Public Building Service, Office of Construction Management, August, 1972.

Light Measurement and Control, Published by the General Electric Company, Large Lamp Department, Nela Park, Cleveland, Ohio, 1971.

"McDonald's Headquarters Building Designed for Open Plan Offices," (Staff Article), *Contract Magazine*, February, 1971, pp. 59–64.

New Technics in Office Operations — Machines, Forms, Systems, Business Equipment Manufacturers Association (BEMA), The Business Press, Elmhurst, Illinois, 1968.

"One New York Plaza Fire," Reported by The New York Board of Fire Underwriters, Bureau of Fire Prevention and Public Relations, 1970.

"One World Trade Center Fire," Reported by The New York Board of Fire Underwriters, Bureau of Fire Prevention and Public Relations, 1975.

"Reducing Lighting Fixtures, Lamps Are not the Solution to the Energy Crunch," *Contract Magazine*, August, 1975, pp. 80–81.

"Technical Series: Workstations with Up and Down Lighting," *Interiors Magazine*, September, 1975, pp. 88–97.

Test Method for the Direct Measurement of Speech-Privacy Potential (SPP) Based on Subject Judgments, General Service Administration, Public Building Service, Office of Construction Management, August, 1972.

Test Method for the Sufficient Verification of Speech-Privacy Potential (SPP) Based on Objective Measurements, General Service Administration, Public Building Service, Office of Construction Management, August, 1972.

The Goal is: Mobility! Published for the National Citizens Conference by the U. S. Department of Health, Education, Welfare, Social and Rehabilitative Service, Washington, D. C. 20201, Doc. No. SRS-113, 1969.

"Waste Not, Watt Not," *Progressive Architecture*, May, 1975, pp. 80–83.